MW00366386

Glad Day

Daily Meditations
for Gay, Lesbian, Bisexual,
and Transgender People

JOAN LARKIN

Hazelden
Publishing

Hazelden Publishing
hazelden.org/bookstore

©1998 by Joan Larkin
Printed in the United States of America
No portion of this publication may be reproduced in any manner without
the written permission of the publisher

Library of Congress Cataloging-in-Publication Data

Larkin, Joan.
   Glad day : daily meditations for gay, lesbian, bisexual, and transgender
people / Joan Larkin.
        p.   cm.
   Includes index.
   ISBN 1–56838–189–1
   1. Gay men—Prayer-books and devotions—English. 2. Lesbians—Prayer-
books and devotions—English. 3. Bisexual—Prayer-books and devotions—
English. 4. Transsexuals—Prayer-books and devotions—English. 5. Twelve-
step programs—Religious aspects—Meditations. 6. Devotional calendars.
I. Title.
BL624.5.L36   1998
   306.76'6—dc21   98–24698
                                                                  CIP

Book design by Will H. Powers
Typesetting by Stanton Publication Services, Inc.
Cover design by David Spohn
19   11

Acknowledgments

I OWE A DEBT OF GRATITUDE to all the people at Hazelden whose vision helped make this book possible. I especially want to thank Kate Kjorlien and Gordon Thomas. Gordon encouraged and worked with me at the beginning; his greatness of heart has touched my own. Kate's clarity, extraordinary patience, and steady guidance have buoyed my spirits throughout.

Heartfelt thanks to dear friend Doug Atwood, for so much more than research; to beloved John Masterson, for insisting on laughter; to Judith Katz, for encouragement at crucial moments; to Shelley McGrew, for a healer's touch and a light spirit; to Stanley Siegel, for insight and caring; and to Kate Larkin, who has always believed in me and said so. And thanks to all the spirited gay, lesbian, bisexual, and transgender people who have shared their vision, experience, and courage, especially those at High Noon, Sundays at the Center.

Help and support from many more than the few I've named here were necessary to the writing of this book. I'm grateful to you all.

Introduction

Glad Day, the title of this book, is a phrase that has often been associated with the movement for gay liberation. It comes from a watercolor painting by William Blake of a dancing boy whose raised arms are outstretched against a background of bright sun. It is an image of morning, new freedom, beginnings, and joy.

The meditations in *Glad Day* are meant to offer a reminder, each day, of the wholeness and beauty of our nature, of the glad spirit that dances in each one of us. Each meditation comes from the belief that as lesbian, gay, bisexual, and transgender people, we have the gift of insight, and the belief that our sexuality, however we have come to understand and define it, can give us access to an awareness of Spirit. Whatever our momentary conflicts, whatever the circumstances of our worlds, nothing need stand between us and the gladness at the source of our lives. Nothing need keep us from the joy that is our essence. We can greet and celebrate it each day.

Since much of my own relationship with Spirit evolves from the transforming experiences of coming out and of recovery, references to both are interwoven throughout these meditations. The Twelve Steps of Alcoholics Anonymous and other anonymous groups are offered at the end of the book; the Twelve Step program is one of the many possible frames of reference for an ongoing daily conversation with Spirit. The choice of a language for that conversation is a personal one. Whatever your own frame of reference, my hope is that these meditations will serve you in your continuing process of transformation.

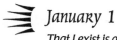 ## January 1

That I exist is a perpetual surprise which is life.

RABINDRANATH TAGORE

Today, I begin again.

I acknowledge and accept my past without regrets or judgments—it has brought me to this moment of beauty, maturity, and possibility. I have learned more about who I am and can embrace my true self with compassion, respect, and tenderness. This day, this year, this moment are new creations, and so is my life. Time is my friend. It may hold miracles of recovery; of a more expansive lesbian, gay, bisexual, or transgender identity; of a richer connection to the spirit within me; of a deeper engagement with friends and community.

I can create a shining day by keeping an open mind, being willing to see myself and others in a new light, and choosing positive responses to experience. I can cultivate new attitudes and visions, accept new opportunities for taking action, and let my voice speak my own truth. I commit myself to keeping creativity and joy alive in my life.

Today, I am alive, enjoying the new creation that is my life.

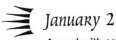 *January 2*

*Armed with scars
healed
in many different colors*

AUDRE LORDE

Shame is learned from an early age. While young, we were alert to subtle and not-so-subtle signals sent by those around us. Whether or not we fully understood our difference, we sensed the threat it posed to others. We tried to be "good," to fit in, to earn the approval of family, friends, teachers, and even of God; we learned the loneliness of pretending to be what we thought others wanted us to be. Some of us turned to addictive substances or behaviors to free ourselves from an existence that cramped our souls. But the price of temporary release was more shame and separation—not just from others, but from self and Spirit.

Turning to the Twelve Steps, we find a path that offers not only freedom from addiction but also the chance to live without shame or denial, the chance to become the people we've always wanted to be. Recovery gives us the opportunity to bring our old, internalized homophobia into the light and let it go. Our Higher Power works to help us in our lives, not to punish us. Self-acceptance includes embracing our sexual selves in a spiritual context.

Today, I cherish my sexuality in all its manifestations: to do so is a spiritual act.

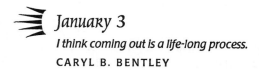

January 3

I think coming out is a life-long process.

CARYL B. BENTLEY

The phrase "coming out," though we sometimes use it to refer simply to our first experience of sexual intimacy with someone of our own gender, has many meanings. We come out to ourselves when we acknowledge the depth and power of our sexual preferences. We come out to others each time we declare ourselves to be gay, lesbian, transgender, or bisexual—or whatever terms we use in creating definitions of ourselves.

Coming out is not something we do just once in our lives, any more than recovery is something we accomplish and complete on the first day we put down an addictive substance or behavior. Coming out is a journey over time. Our experience of it evolves and changes. It's part of the process of getting to know ourselves and of allowing others to know us. Our perceptions of homophobia in our workplaces, families, or communities may affect the extent to which we feel capable of coming out to others at any given time. Whatever our external circumstances, each new day affords us opportunities to understand, accept, and love the people we are, just as we are.

Today, I greet part of myself that I have closed off or denied. I am willing to accept all that I am.

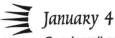

January 4

One doesn't get liberated by hiding. One doesn't possess integrity by passing for "white."

RITA MAE BROWN

Not every situation requires that we identify ourselves to others as lesbian, gay, bisexual, or transgender; there are moments when declaring our sexual identity is simply irrelevant. But what about those times when we are conscious of "passing," or of hiding? We may choose to keep silent when someone makes a homophobic joke or comment, or to keep silent about ourselves when others are sharing about plans or experiences that involve heterosexual partners. There are countless situations in everyday life in which we must choose whether to hide or reveal ourselves. Some of us have cultivated the habit of hiding, telling ourselves it's not worth the risks that may be involved in coming out.

We pay a price for self-censorship. Each day, we have opportunities to keep silent or to speak our truth, to dismiss or acknowledge what matters to us. When we choose to hide from others, we may also be hiding from ourselves and blocking our connection to the spirit within us. We may be cultivating habits of fear and self-rejection. When we know and accept ourselves as we are, we acquire the capacity to make freer choices. As we become more comfortable with ourselves, we can take the risk of letting others know us.

Today, wherever I am, I let the spirit within me shine.

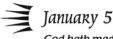 *January 5*

God hath made me to laugh, so that all that hear will laugh with me.

GENESIS 18:12

We sense that recovery is a serious business. It may be the hardest decision we've made in our lives so far. For many of us, acknowledging and choosing to embrace our identity as gay, lesbian, bisexual, or transgender people and to live it fully, without denial, may be an equally difficult choice. As we face and let go of the various kinds of denial that have kept us from seeing ourselves clearly, we needn't feel only struggle and seriousness. We're not alone in surrendering to the truths of addiction and of sexual identity. As we share our experiences with others, we sense more fully what we have lived through. We are freer than we have ever been in our lives. We may share the worst experiences we can imagine, yet hear the laughter of recognition and identification. We can learn from one another to acknowledge the joys of survival, self-awareness, and self-love. We can cultivate laughter in our lives right now, in this moment.

There is no joy like the joy of those who have hit bottom and survived. There is no laughter like the laughter of those who know who they are and embrace life as it is.

Today, I love to laugh.

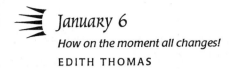

January 6

How on the moment all changes!

EDITH THOMAS

We've discarded old roles and habits; we've grown more confident and comfortable. Still, we don't always feel like celebrating. Fear, anger, sadness— when are we going to be free of "feeling bad"? We all struggle at times with negative feelings. They aren't right or wrong; we don't choose them, and we needn't judge or deny them. However, we can choose how we respond to our feelings. When we're frightened or angry, we can acknowledge what we're experiencing; we don't have to condemn ourselves, act on our feelings, or cling to them. When sadness or grief arises, we can simply sit with our emotions, allowing ourselves to feel them fully. They won't overwhelm or destroy us; in fact, they will pass more quickly and easily than if we reject or stifle them.

Writing, drawing, or other forms of creative expression help us to sense our currents of feeling and allow them to flow through us. When we honor our feelings by greeting them and letting them pass, anger doesn't turn to rage or sadness to despair. Our spirits lighten. Others in our lives perceive that they, too, are safe to feel.

Today, it's safe for me to experience powerful feelings.

January 7

Every man should own at least one dress –
and so should lesbians.

JANE ADAMS

As we've claimed and embraced our identities as
lesbian, gay, bisexual, or transgender people, we
have sought from our communities the acceptance
that family or society may have denied us. We may
have been tempted into new versions of correctness.
Still alert to others' expectations, we may have hidden the quirks and differences that are unique to us
as individuals.

We haven't connected with others only to live
lives of unquestioning conformity. The various
ways we've worked to liberate ourselves—acknowledging our sexual identity or entering recovery, for
example—offer opportunities for self-discovery and
for the courage to be ourselves and love ourselves.
We aren't required to pay the price of sameness,
political correctness, or self-erasure. We haven't
acknowledged parts of ourselves only to deny
other parts. We are entitled to love that goes beyond mere tolerance. No longer numb to our feelings and desires, we can begin to sense that we're
free to make our own maps and to risk following
them.

Today, I embrace an aspect of myself that I've kept
hidden from myself or others.

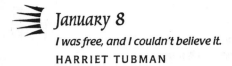

January 8

I was free, and I couldn't believe it.

HARRIET TUBMAN

Coming out to ourselves and others as gay, lesbian, bisexual, or transgender is just a beginning. We've redefined ourselves, freed ourselves from labels that no longer fit. But the habit of disavowing ourselves, our dreams, and our desires may have stayed with us. Perhaps we're still being loyal to the old tradition of thinking we're somehow less important and less worthy than others. Perhaps we habitually try to guess what another person—friend, lover, employer, or family member—wants from us, trying hard to meet what we perceive as others' requirements before identifying or expressing our own.

We can begin to take note of our own visions, wants, and needs and not dismiss them. We can listen attentively and lovingly to the messages that our bodies, our dreams, and our deep, spontaneous feelings are sending us. We can honor our true selves.

Today, I cherish the freedom to define myself and to honor the unique person I am.

 *January 9*

What is sauce for the goose may be sauce for the gander, but is not necessarily sauce for the chicken, the duck, the turkey or the guinea hen.
ALICE B. TOKLAS

Perhaps at times in the past we've engaged in unsafe sex, used sex as an anesthetic, or let others' wants dictate sexual behavior that we ourselves did not want. Perhaps, fearing rejection, we've acted against our own desires; perhaps we haven't even known for certain what our desires were or were not. Exploiting or letting ourselves be exploited in sexual situations rarely brought us the approval we hoped for, and never did it nourish mutual respect or love.

Learning to be true to who we are causes radical changes in our lives. Changes in our sexual lives are possible; with honesty and willingness, we can bring the lessons of recovery into any area of living. Giving ourselves permission to recognize and honor our own sexual feelings is a mark of self-esteem that furthers all other aspects of our lives.

Today, my sexual self deserves to be given my awareness, respect, and love.

January 10

No one has imagined us.

ADRIENNE RICH

We're bombarded by images in newspapers and magazines, in advertisements and on television programs, yet we rarely find ourselves reflected accurately or fully there. In this era of so-called information, the distortion, stereotyping, and often complete absence of representations of our lives in the media may tempt us to doubt the validity of our own experiences. The literature of liberation, spirituality, and Twelve Step recovery helps to illuminate our path; still, it offers only the tools for achieving knowledge of who we are, not the knowledge itself.

Each day, we're blessed with opportunities to get to know ourselves "from scratch"; to face past history and present experience with truthfulness, courage, and the joy of possibility; to look deep within and recognize our true selves. We need no longer be limited by the ways others have defined us as we greet the spirit within us and begin becoming the people we've always wanted to be.

Today, I love the uniqueness and diversity I see around me; I place no conditions on the love I offer myself and others.

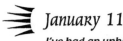 *January 11*

I've had an unhappy life, thank God.

RUSSELL BAKER

We are blessed with the awareness that our past suffering has served a purpose. What we once feared would destroy us has instead led us to understanding and caring, for both ourselves and others. Isolation and loneliness have been replaced by membership in a supportive community. Our experience, strength, and hope are of use to those whose life journeys resemble our own. Survival has given us the gifts of shared laughter and compassion and the courage to take risks and to continue on paths of growth and change.

Whether we've lost everything or have kept whatever luck bestowed on us, each of us has had to change. We've begun learning that we can be fully present in the moment; we no longer fear being alive and awake, as our consciousness of a Higher Power and a loving fellowship sustains us.

Today, I celebrate my strength. I have survived.

 **January 12**

in order to care about you
I have to be everything that is in me

KATE RUSHIN

What exactly are we talking about when we talk about love? Is it merging our lives with another person's life—two people thinking, feeling, and acting in agreement? Is it never again feeling lonely, frightened, angry, or sad? Is it attempting to fill up our own and another person's empty spaces? Is it meeting another person's needs so well that we'll never risk conflict or have to suffer rejection or loss again? Is it finding the "perfect" person?

Our thirst for love may sometimes lead us to deny needs and wants that are important in our development as individuals. Healthy, lasting relationships are not based on lack of self-regard. Learning how to love and honor other human beings begins with exploring and acknowledging our own needs and wants and treating ourselves with compassion, tenderness, and respect. The more room we make for ourselves, the more spacious and generous our love for others becomes.

Today, I take time to focus on ways of loving myself.

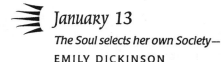

January 13

The Soul selects her own Society—

EMILY DICKINSON

Some of us have open, loving, mutually supportive relationships with our families of origin; some of us are on a long, slow path of amends and reconciliation that we trust will bring healing where there has been conflict and pain; still others may have good reasons for choosing to maintain a healthy distance from our families of origin.

We are discovering profound connections with new friends. We have begun making deep connections based not on the accident of birth or the need for institutional or community approval, but on freedom, mutual trust, and loyalty. We are developing our families of choice and the communities that support and strengthen us.

Today, I am creating a family and community of my choice.

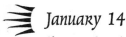

January 14

If you are here to read this,
think of those who aren't . . .
Think of their great sacrifice.

MEL ASH

For every one of us who has recovered from addiction, there are dozens who have gone mad or died or who have denied their dreams. Some have survived merely to lead, in Henry David Thoreau's words, "lives of quiet desperation."

When we think of the sickness, suffering, and despair of those who have died or who are still active in their addictions, our response need not be moral judgment, survivor's guilt, or denial. We can feel compassion for them as well as for those—including ourselves—on whom their lives have had an impact. We can acknowledge that others have been a part of our own path to recovery and thank them in our hearts. We can recognize how little separates our lives from theirs. We can appreciate life's fragility and riskiness, rejoice in the freedom recovery affords, and commit ourselves to becoming all we can be in the time we've been given. We can enfold those who still suffer in the love and warmth of our thoughts, praying that they achieve peace.

Today, I feel my connection to all those
who are suffering, and I pray for their well-being.

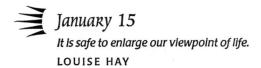

January 15

It is safe to enlarge our viewpoint of life.

LOUISE HAY

Most of us—even though we may now take pride in ourselves as lesbian, gay, bisexual, or transgender people and sense support from our new families and communities—still carry the psychic weight of a partly negative self-image. It is uncomfortable work to carry this weight. Without that burden, our spirits are free to become their original shining selves, free to expand, laugh, dance, and savor life.

Imagine what would happen if we were to let go of every negative or limiting idea we still hold about ourselves. We would refuse to deny, stereo-type, or reject any aspect of our beings. We would view with love and compassion all that has hap-pened in the past and all that is encompassed by our present situation in life. Each of us would wrap our entire self—our body, our unique gifts and so-called shortcomings, and our wildest fears and dreams—with loving thoughts.

We are capable of even greater love for ourselves and others than we have yet imagined.

Today, I radiate unconditional love.

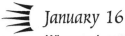 *January 16*

*Whoever degrades another degrades me, and
    whatever is done or said returns at last to me,
And whatever I do or say I also return.*

WALT WHITMAN

At times we feel profoundly alone. Although we've
begun to understand the depth and importance of
our connection to other human beings, that connection can still elude us. Some of us feel anger, remembering ways we may have been treated by family,
teachers, employers, mates, or acquaintances. Some
of us feel guilt and regret about our own behavior
toward others. As we work the Twelve Steps and
feel supported and included by new friends in recovery, our hearts expand; we reach out to others,
sharing our experience, strength, and hope. Over
time, we begin to feel compassion for our former
selves and even for those we believe harmed us.

Anger and shame don't end just because we
enter recovery, but today we don't have to react
with words or actions that disparage others. When
negative feelings arise, we now can be conscious of
the impact of what we say and do.

*Today, I speak and act consciously,
with respect for myself and others.*

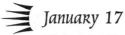 *January 17*

> *We had developed a genuine relationship
> based on truth, not on the rules and roles
> that fathers and daughters were expected
> to play for each other.*

STANLEY SIEGEL

Some of us have children in our lives. We may wonder when is the right time to come out to them or to let them know that we're in recovery. Shouldn't we protect them from sensitive information that they may be too young to handle?

Who we are is apparent to those close to us. Children usually have an intuitive awareness of the truths that we may have taken elaborate pains to try to conceal, telling ourselves that we're doing so for their protection. There are no universal rules about how or when to come out to children and others in our lives; what's appropriate varies from situation to situation. Often it's our own reluctance, rather than others' ability to hear and accept the truth, that keeps us from speaking.

When we speak the truth, we must be willing to listen to truthful responses. We can listen with understanding and acceptance even to negative reactions, knowing that what someone feels free to express can change. Rather than losing the people in our lives, we may be surprised to experience far greater honesty, trust, and closeness in our relationships than we had imagined possible.

*Today, I have the courage to tell the truth
in my relationships.*

January 18

I study because I must.

SOR JUANA INÉS DE LA CRUZ

We're free to make choices and to create change in all aspects of our lives, inner and outer. We can embark on new learning, seek education and meaningful work, take positive steps to improve and maintain physical and mental health, experience fulfillment in relationships, and pursue a spiritual path.

Addiction and denial can put dreams on hold. Old fears and judgments still invite us to listen; they say things like "It's too late" or "You can't afford it" or "What makes you think you can do *that*?" But when our own or others' thoughts of negativity and limitation speak through us, we can recognize that they are simply thoughts and that thoughts can change. We don't have to remain loyal to old habits of self-rejection. We are willing to bring about change and growth in our lives, and knowing that is a source of joy.

Today, I'm open to new learning.
I take steps to make the positive changes I desire.

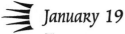 *January 19*

There were no role models for female singer-songwriters when I began in the early sixties and fewer for young lesbians.

JANIS IAN

As gay, lesbian, bisexual, and transgender people, we may have the sense that the recorded history of others like us has many gaps. Without role models, we may opt for the safety of trying to appear to be "like everyone else," taking our notions of who we are and should be from heterosexual culture. Sensing our difference, we may be tempted to consider ourselves inadequate, somehow defective.

Finding out who we are, who we need and want to become, is vital to the process of our recovery. We must cultivate relationships with those whose lives inspire us with courage, truthfulness, and self-respect—role models whose examples show us how to thrive as our authentic selves. And we have a responsibility to be ourselves, willing to be seen by others as role models who are both sober and proud.

Today, I am responsible for being myself, whether or not I am like anyone else I have met so far.

 ## January 20

Beauty is the love that we devote to an object.

PAUL SÉRUSIER

What we find beautiful is not a trivial matter in our lives. Beauty, wherever we experience it, can be nourishment, relaxation, stimulation, healing, appetite, variety, individual choice, aliveness, or awe. Color, rhythm, scent, and texture are elements of everything we encounter, from food to music to books to sexual expression. The beauty of spareness speaks to some, the beauty of abundance to others.

The beauty we find in nature, whether we're seeing dramatic ocean waves or single drops of water, awakens and restores us. The beauty we create in our home and work environments expresses deep needs of our soul at any given time in our development. The unique beauty of each of our bodies, faces, rhythms of moving and speaking, visions and dreams, and journeys of growth and unfolding can be as beautiful as anything else in this world.

Our spirits are fulfilled and satisfied by the many forms of beauty that reverberate through our lives.

Today, I delight in my gift for experiencing beauty.

 *January 21*

*They are slaves who fear to speak for the fallen
and the weak.*

J. R. LOWELL

Having experienced our own liberation, we cannot
be indifferent to others whose struggles and journeys so closely resemble our own. We know that we
have to "give it away to keep it"; to share our experience, strength, and hope; to give service; to reach
out; and to be a powerful example to those still suffering. From our experiences as lesbian, gay, bisexual, or transgender people, we have benefited from
the courage and outspokenness of others like ourselves. We have come a long distance on the path of
self-acknowledgment, self-acceptance, and celebration of our identities. A vital part of our maturity is
having the courage to care and speak for others in
need.

*Today, I speak with the courage
that comes from self-esteem.*

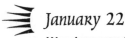

January 22

Way down yonder by myself,
oh I couldn't hear nobody pray.

AFRICAN AMERICAN SPIRITUAL

Most of us have experienced, at some time or another, how a simple word of encouragement from another person can suddenly ease our labor. We may have been struggling under the burden of what seemed like an insurmountable task, weighed down by fear, depression, shame, or self-hate. Simple words of reassurance from one other person were all it took to turn us around. Hearing positive words from another gave us faith and confidence. We felt comforted, enlivened, and motivated to continue our efforts.

We, too, have the ability to make a difference by speaking simple words of encouragement. We only need to remember how far we have come and to trust the capacity of our spirits to grow and expand in unexpected and positive directions.

Today, I speak simple words of encouragement
to others and to myself.

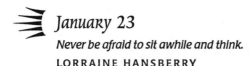

January 23

Never be afraid to sit awhile and think.

LORRAINE HANSBERRY

Those of us who have experienced cravings and compulsions have at times felt we had no choice but to use an addictive substance or behavior. Resolutions, promises, plans, others' needs, our own dreams and desires—nothing could stop us from acting on our compulsion. Guilt and shame followed, as we knew they would. Sometimes remorse slowed down our using for a while—until the next time.

Recovery offers tools that enable us to stop and think through the consequences of an action we may feel tempted to take. Whether it's picking up our primary addiction or engaging in behavior that feels out of sync with our lives in recovery— telling lies, keeping secrets, indulging in character assassination—we don't have to act instantly. We can call a trusted friend or sponsor, attend a meeting, read recovery literature, share with others, or pray. The same is true when the prospect of something positive arises. We needn't rush into a new job or relationship. We can give ourselves time to test the waters, see how we feel, and think through the consequences of our actions.

Today, I'm not in a rush to take actions or make commitments. I can allow myself time to think.

 ## January 24

*First noticed in the early 1980's, . . . AIDS has had
dramatic effects on virtually every aspect of gay
and lesbian life.*

STEVE HOGAN AND LEE HUDSON

Whether we ourselves, our friends, or members of
our families and communities are living with HIV
or AIDS, our lives have been and continue to be affected by the profound changes wrought by this
epidemic. For many of us, contemplating AIDS
brings only a sense of fear, loss, or overwhelming
catastrophe. While not denying the depths of our
grief, we can also recognize how AIDS has opened
doors to new ways of life.

Our communities have responded by creating
hundreds of organizations that engage in research,
service, education, counseling, and personal assistance. The epidemic has stirred us to extraordinary
levels of political activity; has improved communication and teamwork among lesbian, gay, bisexual,
and transgender people; and has inspired compassion in and involvement by many heterosexuals.
Many of us have found greater stability and loyalty in our relationships and more powerful ways
of expressing our spirituality. Many have learned
that to be tender and devoted to one another is an
authentic and a deeply healing part of who we are.

*Today, I focus on all that is alive, expressive,
and healing in my life.*

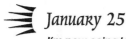 *January 25*

*I'm now going to say something that may
surprise you.* Death can be very inspiring.

SOGYAL RINPOCHE

At some point, we all must face the death of one
we care about. We're used to thinking only in terms
of the pain and sadness of loss. But if we have the
privilege of spending time with a dying person, we
may be surprised to find ourselves uplifted by the
experience.

When we're at a loss for what to do in the face of
suffering, we can let our hearts expand with compassion, trusting in the presence of a Higher Power
as we pray for others to be free of mental and physical pain. If the person is able to speak and needs to
give voice to fears, guilt, or regrets, we can listen
attentively. Even if the dying person can no longer
communicate through speech, he or she may still be
able to hear us. We can speak appreciatively about
all the good his or her life has brought into being.

When we visit the dying with encouraging, open
hearts, a powerful atmosphere of generosity and inspiration can result.

*Today, my compassion for myself and others
transforms fear into faith.*

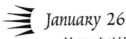 *January 26*

*i beg what i love and
i leave to forgive me.*
LUCILLE CLIFTON

When a loving relationship comes to an end, we don't have to view the ending as a failure. It is not a failure when separation comes after we've understood that fundamental needs and wants cannot be met in the relationship. We have done our best. We have soberly and maturely faced the truth of our need to move apart. We have communicated this as openly and lovingly as we can. We can count this ending not as a failure, but as a success.

Whether we experience an ending as something we ourselves have chosen or as the result of another person's decision, we will have to experience our feelings of grief. At first, we may feel only anger; underneath may be the pain of loss. If we allow our feelings to surface and don't deny or deaden them, we'll be surprised at how easily we're able to let them go. We'll feel our hearts expand and make room for love, both from ourselves and from others.

Today, I delight in my honest, loving relationship with myself.

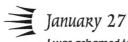 **January 27**

I was ashamed to admit the extent of our violence.

KATE HURLEY

Some of us are involved in relationships character-ized by violence, some of it overt, some of it subtle, all of it destructive to spiritual growth. Whether we're perpetrators or victims of violence, and whether the violence is physical or psychological, we need to stop perpetuating it.

Denial, shame, or fear of loss—loss of a relation-ship or loss of community approval and support—may keep us from speaking about our role in a violent relationship. Various forms of violence are more common among us than we have been willing to acknowledge. Any of us who have experienced battering or abuse at some time in the past and any of us who suffer from self-hatred or who have used addictive substances or behaviors to numb feelings of outrage and frustration are at risk.

Speaking aloud with a trusted person can be a first step toward awareness and acceptance. It is necessary to bring the existence of violence out into the open before it can be healed.

Today, I can safely speak about shame.
I begin the process of healing.

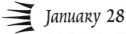

January 28

Relationships, I believe, are truly sacred, not in the superficial meaning of simply being high in value, but in that they call upon infinite and mysterious depths in ourselves, in our communities, and in the very nature of things.

THOMAS MOORE

Perhaps we have been loyal to a partner in a long-term primary relationship. Perhaps we have had wide and varied sexual or romantic experience and regard ourselves as sophisticated, or even jaded. Perhaps we feel lonely, ambivalent, or awkward and can't imagine how to begin meeting potential partners. We may only recently have begun to perceive ourselves as gay, lesbian, bisexual, or transgender.

As we gain a clearer awareness of our feelings, we can refrain from instant judgments and actions based on the way we feel at each moment. Let's allow ourselves as much time as we need and treat ourselves with gentleness and respect as we gradually come to understand and appreciate our own particular needs and preferences.

Today, I cultivate a loving relationship with myself. I completely accept myself just as I am right now.

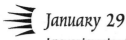 *January 29*

I never imagined myself as ordinary.

JOE ORTON

Many controversies thread through gay, lesbian, bi-sexual, and transgender life. How are we to keep our serenity, let alone discover the truth of our own needs and preferences, amid all the conflict within our communities?

Instead of feeling pressured to side with certain factions and criticize others, we can ask ourselves what we ourselves believe and value. Why are we so concerned with others' opinions? If we're not yet comfortable with our own identities, we may be attracted to the apparent safety of rules. When we know and accept ourselves, we are not likely to be unnerved by conflict. We can speak our own truth even in the face of opposition. Let's make getting to know and express our true selves a higher priority than seeking others' approval.

Today, I feel safe to acknowledge my true feelings and preferences, whether or not they are in fashion.

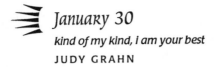 *January 30*

kind of my kind, i am your best

JUDY GRAHN

When we love someone of the same gender, we sometimes feel as if we've merged completely: the thin boundaries separating one body from another, one consciousness from another, seem to have dissolved. We're in ecstasy, intoxicated with the sense of oneness.

But a total melting of boundaries may also bring fear, even panic. Does loving and being loved mean we have to sacrifice the sense of who we are and what we want? We may feel as if we're lost and wonder how we'll ever get ourselves back. To feel safe again, we may assert our need for boundaries abruptly or unkindly, even in ways that threaten the very connection we desire.

If we're to survive the chaotic swirl of developing intimacy, it's essential that we learn to identify and share the truth of our feelings. Speaking honestly, without blaming ourselves or another person, allows us to feel both safe and intimate as we merge and separate over and over in a loving relationship.

Today, I have the courage to speak my truth
in a way that considers the feelings of others.

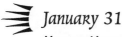 *January 31*

I have not been able to touch the destruction within me.

AUDRE LORDE

We can still see examples of homophobia almost everywhere we look: in families, communities, laws, and institutions. We've heard public figures, including elected officials, refer to us as "sick," "immoral," or "unnatural." Many of us have lost homes, promotions, custody battles, and even people we thought of as friends as the result of such homophobic attitudes.

Sadness, anger, creative expression, and activism are among our many responses toward the bias and bigotry we encounter. But what about our own homophobia? Even those of us who are most outspoken have absorbed and internalized prevailing homophobic attitudes. At some level perhaps deeper than our conscious awareness, we may still blame, disparage, or denigrate ourselves. We may have used addictive substances or behaviors to numb the pain of self-rejection. Each of us must face our internalized homophobia before complete healing can take place in our hearts and in our families and communities.

Today, I confront my own homophobia as I grow in self-love and self-acceptance.

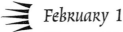 ## February 1

*When we meet someone, we say, "Hello, cousin,"
or "Hello, Grandfather." And this is not merely
symbolic, but a reminder that we have a family.*

GENE THIN ELK

In our need and enthusiasm for declaring loyalty
to new supportive communities and families of our
own choice, we may forget that we are part of the
larger human family. This family includes children
and old people. It includes those whose gender or
sexual orientation differs from ours. It includes
members of other groups that experience oppression, as well as people whose lives we consider
privileged—those we assume have no experience
of suffering comparable to our own. All are worthy
of our compassion.

In recovery programs, we discover people who
seem different from us but who share with us feelings and experiences common to those living with
addiction. As we look around us and acknowledge
a variety of other people, as we pray for the well-
being of those whom we know and those whom we
don't know, our spirits grow. Our narrow definitions of kin and community expand to include all
members of the human family.

*Today, I affirm with love my connection
to the human family.*

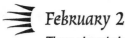 February 2

There almost always is a discrepancy in . . . timing for a gay man, because there are no sanctions and approvals for his exploring his sexuality when everyone else is, during chronological adolescence.

STANLEY SIEGEL

We may have sensed from an early age that our sexual identity was different from the one validated by our families and the larger community. Or we may be just beginning to explore a bisexual, lesbian, gay, or transgender identity. Wherever we are in the process of getting to know our sexual natures, we may have feelings or experiences that seem incongruous with our mature selves.

We needn't expect ourselves to know everything today. As we grow, progress, and learn new skills at our own pace, our sense of who we really are expands and deepens. We can learn from those who have already been there, and we can mentor others who are at more awkward stages than we are. We can allow ourselves to have mixed feelings and to make mistakes; both are useful teachers. We stay loving and patient with ourselves at every stage.

Today, I praise and support myself in my unique process of development.

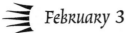

February 3

This is my poetic son.

A mother introducing her nine-year-old son
to a friend at the first National AIDS March,
quoted by Stanley Siegel

We wish parents and others in roles of responsibility toward children were more commonly open to and accepting of the natural diversity of sexual identities. We long for the time when self-esteem will be fostered by society's complete acceptance and respect for lesbian, gay, bisexual, and transgender people. We imagine a day when all parents will keep their children safe from the dangers of ignorance and bigotry.

Such a future will come about only if we accept the naturalness of our sexual identities, the dignity of our lives, the strength of our spirits, and the necessity for our full inclusion if the human family is to remain whole and healthy. We have a responsibility to our own and others' children to view ourselves as we want others to view us—with generosity, openness, and respect.

*Today, I increase tolerance in the world
by offering understanding to myself and others.*

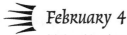

February 4

It's hard to give away much when you're the subject of widespread disapproval and your heart is leaking from puncture wounds.

BARBARA KINGSOLVER

Anger doesn't necessarily vanish just because we've come out or entered recovery. Our best selves would like to be generous to the employer who overlooks us for a promotion, to the old friend who tells us we could change if we'd just set our minds to it, and to the family that asks, "Where did we go wrong?" We're sick of our old conflicts and resentments, but our anger and sense of injury keep overwhelming our desire to let go.

We need to find safe ways to acknowledge anger and to release the pain it may be covering. A trusted sponsor, a Twelve Step recovery meeting, or a therapist can hear us without denying or condemning our emotions. When we recognize, accept, and express our anger without judging it, we'll be surprised at the mental and spiritual space we've created for new feelings.

Today, I don't have to act out my anger.
I acknowledge it and let it pass through me.

February 5

If you, as an adult, lived with someone who was as abusive to you as you are to your body, you would have the option of moving out. Your body has no such choice. Day after day it suffers your remarks, your grimaces, and your endless attacks on its size and shape.

JANE HIRSCHMANN
AND CAROL MUNTER

As difficult as it is to live up to certain standards—whether set by mainstream culture or by the communities we've chosen to call our own—we may not be ready to question those standards. We may habitually condemn our age, size, shape, or appearance without challenging cultural ideals or our own negative self-image.

Obsession with cultural judgments about how bodies should look can be a socially acceptable cover for other forms of self-rejection that we'd prefer to avoid acknowledging. Staying preoccupied with our failure to have "perfect" bodies can be an effective way to keep us from thinking our real thoughts and feeling our real desires. Letting go of negative self-judgments liberates energy and willingness to care lovingly for our bodies and our authentic selves.

Today, I see my body's unique beauty and listen to its needs. I care for it as its most loving friend.

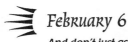 *February 6*

And don't just ask for one mercy.
Let them flood in.

RUMI

Perhaps we've allowed feelings of disappointment or discouragement to take root in us. We may have decided to settle for less than our dreams, blaming the past or other people for our present dissatisfaction. We may cling to the belief that if we give up, we will somehow be taken care of. We must not give in to self-doubt or cynicism and misname it "acceptance." If we dream of pursuing education, meaningful work, a loving relationship, creative expression, spiritual practice, or something else we deeply desire, we can cultivate hope as we take steps toward our goal.

Twelve Step recovery reminds us that while we don't have the power to change others, we *can* affect our own lives by changing our attitudes and by taking actions. Faith in a Higher Power and the willingness to do our part are foundations for change. Open-mindedness, persistence, and patience can bring us closer to understanding and honoring ourselves, at any age, in any aspect of our lives.

Today, I see doors that are open;
I walk through them with faith in my life's abundance.

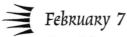 ## February 7

*Ah, well, it was not the first time in my life that
I had gone to bed with a book.*

JEANNE ADLEMAN

Having acknowledged our sexual identities, having
taken risks in coming out to loved ones, employers,
and community members, and having given our energy and enthusiasm to activist causes, we may nevertheless find ourselves without an intimate sexual
relationship.

Periods of celibacy, whether chosen or imposed
by circumstance, can be rich experiences, full of opportunities for freedom, growth, and pleasure. Now
is the time to appreciate the riches of friendship and
of solitude. Now is the time to savor music, reading,
exercise, and meditation; to write or make art; to
create home environments that reflect our personal
taste. Now is the time to focus on a program of recovery or therapy, to take inventories of our sexual
feelings and behavior, or to address spiritual challenges we have been postponing.

*Today, whether or not I am participating in a
sexual partnership, I embrace myself and
affirm my sexual identity.*

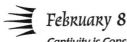

February 8

Captivity is Consciousness—
So's Liberty.

EMILY DICKINSON

Opinions, reactions, criticisms, regrets—from morning till night, our thoughts spin the fabric of our day. We listen as if powerless as thoughts free or torment us, energize us or weigh us down. They may talk about shame, fear, and resentment—or pride, faith, and gratitude. Instead of letting ourselves be controlled by the ceaseless voices in our heads, we remind ourselves of our options. We can sit in meditation, noticing the flow of thoughts and gently detaching from them. We can change our negative thinking, deliberately focusing on images of comfort, courage, and healing. We choose to give such positive thoughts our attention, letting them fill us with hope and serenity. We can receive help with releasing negative thoughts by talking with a trusted friend or sponsor or attending a recovery meeting.

Today, I am nourished and supported by positive thoughts. I choose my thoughts as I do my friends, staying with those I find uplifting.

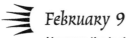 *February 9*

Unscrew the locks from the doors!
Unscrew the doors themselves from their jambs!
WALT WHITMAN

For some, coming out as gay, lesbian, bisexual, or transgender may have been the most difficult and courageous thing we have ever done. For others, acknowledging an addiction and the need for recovery has been the most significant decision of our lives so far. In either case, we've freed ourselves from traditions of thinking and behaving that many people take for granted. We've challenged long-held values and habits. We've had the wisdom to redefine ourselves in ways that feel truer to who we are. We've started on a path of personal liberation.

Such fundamental change can seem overwhelming at first. It's not unusual for old feelings and fears to rise up and briefly make their power felt, just when we thought we had let go of them forever. Knowing that doubt often surfaces in the course of a transformation, we can be patient with ourselves and our process of change. We needn't give up. We need never go back to old, limiting behaviors.

Today, I weather any doubts or fears that accompany transformation. I trust that I am where I'm supposed to be.

February 10

I am a child of seven, returning home from a class-mate's birthday party. I . . . hold out my hand to my mother, revealing a cup of sweets. . . . "It's for you, Mommy," I say—proving, yet again, that I am a good boy, eager to deprive myself to make her happy. In the cup are a variety of candies, nuts, and raisins, all for her; there's nothing for me, no homosexuality in the cup, only a son's love for his mother, who has declared him her personal prop-erty, which he, in his innocence, has accepted as how it should be.

CHARLES SILVERSTEIN

For whom are we living our lives? To what tradi-tions do we remain loyal, and at what price? What beliefs about what others want still keep us from being entirely ourselves?

We are no longer dependent children. Survival skills we once believed we needed are no longer necessary. It's time to stop trying to be what we think others expect. Our Higher Power doesn't ask us to hate any part of ourselves. And we may be underestimating others we love if we assume that they won't continue to love us when we claim and celebrate our true selves.

Today, I can safely become all I am meant to be.

February 11

*It should be clear to all lesbians that ageism
distracts us from the pursuit of our essential Self,
the very identity which lesbianism makes possible.*

BABA COPPER

Each of us goes through many stages from youth to
old age. If we reject anyone because of age, we reject part of ourselves and part of the human condition. We may have opened our hearts and minds to
the diversity surrounding us, but we may still retain
a few of the limiting beliefs that helped shape our
former lives. When we see others in our community
through the lens of ageism, we are also seeing ourselves through the same nearsighted lens: all hatred
is self-hatred, all rejection is self-rejection.

While we have the right to associate with others
who are on our particular wavelength and who
have evolved to a similar place of development, our
vision and growth are enhanced when we include
people of various ages in some aspect of our lives.
It's our responsibility to see that our communities
meet the needs of people of all ages.

Today, I affirm what is beautiful about every age.

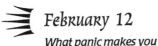 **February 12**

*What panic makes you
want to die?*

JAMES BALDWIN

The presence in our lives of love, success, growth,
abundance, and recovery may disturb us. Such positive change may contradict what we once expected
for ourselves.

Doubt, fear, and the urge for self-sabotage aren't
unusual when we begin experiencing profound
changes for the good. It's tempting to lapse into old
thinking and old behavior patterns that, although
they're uncomfortable, are at least familiar to us.
But we needn't surrender to self-destructive impulses. At such moments we can slow down and
take deep breaths. We can acknowledge the darkness we've put behind us, affirming that our Higher
Power does not wish us to return to it. Rather than
acting on fear and doubt, we can talk with others
who've been there and who remind us to believe in
ourselves and in our Higher Power's unconditional
love for us. We can remain still for a time and absorb the sense of how far we've come. We can then
continue moving forward on our chosen path.

*Today, I needn't let fear or doubt take charge of my
thinking. I keep breathing and look toward the light.*

February 13

Real generosity toward the future consists in giving all to what is present.

ALBERT CAMUS

Years are made up of days, and days of moments. We sometimes imagine dramatic changes we'd like to bring about in our lives overnight. But we must remember that who we are today is the result of a process—a process that has evolved gradually through many small actions taken over time.

Grand flights and gestures occur more often in our fantasies than in our real lives. Though some of us may be able to point to a single, memorable moment of clarity and decision that has transformed us, most awakenings result from our having taken a series of steps over time. The spiritual awakening spoken of in recovery programs is one such process. Our awareness, acceptance, and affirmation of a gay, lesbian, bisexual, or transgender identity is another.

The pleasure of immersion in the present, of appreciation for the details, and of staying in touch with our senses and the flow of our feelings is a gift. Patience isn't something we have to strive for, if we allow ourselves to take life one day at a time.

Today, I am calm and patient with the process of my life. I trust my Higher Power's timetable.

 **February 14**

Love
like anybody else, comes to those who
wait actively

JUDY GRAHN

The songs and films of mainstream culture abound
in images of romantic love. Defining ourselves as
lesbian, gay, bisexual, or transgender doesn't automatically grant us immunity from these images.
Many of us have absorbed the myth that when Mr.
or Ms. Right comes along, emptiness will be filled
and loneliness will be over. The long-awaited romantic relationship will define and complete us.

We don't have to wait for love to come and save
us. We have the ability to have loving relationships
right now with friends, members of our chosen families, and ourselves. We can use the energy of love to
create art, music, or writing; to give service to those
in our communities and recovery programs; and to
deepen our connection to a Higher Power. Secure in
our capacity for love, we can explore new relationships through the process of dating, gradually getting to know others, and allowing ourselves to be
known as we really are.

Today, I give love generously and let it
come back to me.

February 15

*Know that your brother's life
was not what you imagined.*

MICHAEL LASSELL

It may be tempting, once we've committed ourselves to a profound change in our lives, to think
that we know what others, too, ought to do to heal
or grow. We want our friends and loved ones to experience the same relief and joy, the same freedom,
that we're experiencing. We forget that we ourselves
have often resisted advice. No one could have told
us who we were, what to do, or when to do it. Enormous changes such as coming out or entering recovery are deeply personal choices, and the timing of a
decision is individual and delicate.

What's exactly right for us at this particular moment in time may not be at all right for someone
else. Instead of judging another's needs and choices,
we can cultivate sensitivity to the ways that his or
her path or rate of unfolding may differ from our
own. The more secure we are in our own identities,
the easier it is to allow others to be who they are.

Today, I live and lovingly let live.

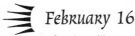 *February 16*

I fear he will prove the weeping philosopher when he grows old, being so full of unmannerly sadness in his youth.

WILLIAM SHAKESPEARE

Having come out—and for some of us, having entered recovery—we may feel a special pressure to perform well and to look good to others. We may have a new sense of how important our tasks and problems are today. Perhaps we even associate playfulness, exuberance, or spontaneity with a lack of dignity or sobriety. We're not sure it's such a good idea to take ourselves any less seriously, let alone to be willing to make fools of ourselves as we risk new experiences.

We can make the decision to keep laughter alive in the course of each day. Our capacity to shed our self-consciousness and have fun is a precious gift. It allows us to appreciate the humor in our mistakes and imperfections, to forgive ourselves and others, and to ride out troubles with a lighter heart. It nurtures our spirits and helps us to move forward in our process of growth. It frees us to be more creative. It gladdens others whose lives are touched by ours.

Today, my enthusiasm and sense of humor lift my own and others' spirits.

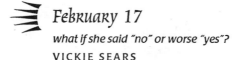

Fᴇʙʀᴜᴀʀʏ 17

what if she said "no" or worse "yes"?

VICKIE SEARS

Even as we progress on our journey of self-realization, even as we learn to understand our deepest desires, we may have a constant fear of taking the next step. Perhaps we've come to define ourselves as lesbian, gay, bisexual, or transgender or to acknowledge our need for a program of recovery only after a long and difficult process. Though we're now at peace about such definitions, we may still balk at what further growth and healing may require of us.

We may be hovering on the brink of a decision about whether or not to move forward. We may hesitate to open ourselves further in an intimate relationship or to ask for greater responsibility and recognition in a work situation. We may want to take a risk in a creative project but fear losing what equilibrium we've gained.

Whatever the question, the answer lies within each of us. No one has the power to free or to imprison our spirits. The decision to turn all concerns over to the care of a loving Higher Power liberates us to take the next step on the journey.

Today, I have the courage to take a step into the unknown.

February 18

We were special to the Sioux, Cheyenne, Ponca
And the Crow who valued our worth.

MAURICE KENNY

Gay, lesbian, bisexual, and transgender people are
not entirely new to the human family, although we
have not always been seen, let alone celebrated, as
"two-spirited" gay Native Americans have been.
Whether or not our predecessors, living in contexts
that differed from our own, defined or experienced
themselves as we do, we can be sure that we're not
the first of our kind under the sun.

Many of us are doing historical and cultural research that has begun to deepen our sense of connection to our roots and to one another. Many are
helping to make sure that we are no longer skipped
over and left out of documentaries, health studies,
textbooks, institutions, news media, films, and
archives.

We, too, can add to this growing fabric of knowledge by remembering, witnessing, and sharing our
own and others' experiences with respect and care
for the truth. Each of us has a contribution to make.
The more we know of our roots, ourselves, and one
another, the more we can truly celebrate who we are.

Today, I bear witness to my own and others' experience,
past and present.

February 19

Try not to force your idea on someone, but rather think about it with him. . . . Try not to win in the argument; just listen to it; but it is also wrong to behave as if you had lost.

SHUNRYU SUZUKI

Sometimes it feels as if our entire lives are made up of dissent and difference. As gay, lesbian, bisexual, or transgender people, we are apt to be acutely aware of our differences from those around us. Wherever we go—even in Twelve Step meetings where we and others speak of our common problem of addiction—we may find ourselves focusing on the ways we are different.

What would happen if we stopped having to prove our point, convincing ourselves or others with repeated arguments? What would happen if we stopped making ourselves or others right or wrong for beliefs and opinions?

Instead of giving our energy to argument, we can simply state our truths and focus on living as if we believed them. Our example of open-mindedness and clarity has more power of persuasion than our efforts to convert others to our point of view.

Today, I keep an open mind in the ongoing process of discovering and expressing what is true for me.

February 20

How long will the bed that we made together hold us there?

TIMOTHY LIU

Some of us see long-term relationships as the ultimate expression of love. We may choose to make a commitment to an exclusive partnership, even to marry one another. Others may prefer looser but equally powerful ties based on mutual trust and need rather than on the traditions of heterosexual marriage. Some of us are creating our own complex, original maps of relationships that reflect our freedom and uniqueness.

Whether we are involved in a primary loving relationship or haven't yet begun to develop social lives that include dating, we can't acknowledge our deepest desires or chart our intended course if an addictive substance or behavior keeps us from living fully in the present. We can't let drug addiction, romantic obsession, or sexual compulsion take the place of the work of learning to know ourselves and others. Free of addiction, we can come out of the isolation and fantasy of the past and choose healthy ways of relating to others.

Today, I'm free to create loving relationships that reflect my true desires.

February 21

*An avalanche of love
has come my way
since I got sick.*

TIM DLUGOS

Stereotypes have portrayed gay, lesbian, bisexual, and transgender people as selfish, sex-obsessed, lonely, and spiritually debased. While we, like all members of the human family, have our share of character defects, we have also shown ourselves capable of unconditional love, generosity, and great tenderness. We have bonded as a family to promote one another's health and healing. We are living with loss after loss, caused by such things as AIDS and breast cancer.

Many spiritual disciplines have taught that the meaning and purpose of our lives is expressed in loving one another. Epidemics of illnesses such as AIDS and breast cancer test our endurance, but also tap into our vast potential to love. We have not had to stop and think about what our response should be. We have discovered our deep and inexhaustible flow of love. We deserve to surround ourselves with it, to give it, and to receive it.

Today, love flows through me.

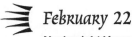 **February 22**

You're right I brought a grain
*   or two of sand*
into bed.

MAY SWENSON

When a situation disturbs our serenity, we needn't
linger long on an old path of anger, blame, and resentment. Instead, we can look at the ways we may
be contributing to our own discomfort, knowing
that it's in our power to change any behavior or
attitude.

   There are always alternatives. We can refuse to
take the stance of victim or martyr. We can speak
up courageously about injustice toward ourselves
or others. We can keep an open mind and acknowledge whatever we are responsible for, make amends
if appropriate, and take steps toward changing our
conduct in the present. We can meditate or share
our feelings with someone we trust, and we can be
willing to let uncomfortable emotions go when they
are ready to leave. We can cultivate gratitude for
the gift of life and for the opportunity to grow in
any situation.

Today, I am not a victim.

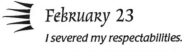 ## February 23

I severed my respectabilities.

JAMES BROUGHTON

We've come a long way on our journeys. We have had to let go of parts of the past in order to live today. We've had to free ourselves of old associations: people, places, and things that can't accept or support us as we know ourselves to be, whether as gay, lesbian, bisexual, or transgender or as people recovering from addictive substances or behaviors.

As our healing and continuing growth require us to change some of our former loyalties and behaviors, we may experience a sense of loss or of doubt. We may wonder if our new life is worth the pain of letting go, of risking the unknown. Though we yearn for unconditional love, we may still seek approval from people and institutions we've left behind. We may consider retreating into old roles and behaviors.

"Cleaning house" is part of taking responsibility for our lives. It isn't always comfortable, but it's necessary for spiritual growth.

Today, my life reflects the values I cherish.
I give myself wholehearted approval.

February 24

I've trust enough in all
that's happened in my life,
the unexpected love
and gentleness that rushes in
to fill the arid spaces
in my heart.

TIM DLUGOS

We sometimes think that it's up to us to solve whatever problems we encounter and to find immediate
solutions. We forget the humility of trust: trust that
we're not in charge of everything, trust in others'
capacity for healing in their own time and in their
own way, trust in our own capacity to receive the
love and sustenance in which our world abounds.

Our spirits thrive, not because we've found a reason for everything or because we've gotten our own
way at last, but because at least for this moment
we've surrendered. Our Higher Power's guidance
will take us on the next step of the journey. This day
will sustain and surprise us.

Trust that you're exactly where you're supposed
to be.

Today, I trust the process of my life.

February 25

*Solitude is . . . when you marry your thoughts. It's
when you start off on the wrong leg and end up
on the right. It's peaceful. It's not languid. It can
make your guts feel as if they are consuming you.
It can be the highlight of the tension which challenges a former truth.*

JULIE NEWMAR

We may think there's something wrong with solitude, equating being alone with loneliness. But we
can choose to make a period of solitude part of the
day, making a commitment to be fully present and
alive, reveling in the time for confiding in ourselves
and paying attention to the Spirit that sustains life.

We can make a list of some uses of solitude we
find pleasurable. Pursuits that may enrich our solitude include writing in a journal, listening to music,
preparing ourselves a favorite meal, reading, taking
a walk or bicycle ride, working on a creative project, studying one of the Twelve Steps, or simply sitting and appreciating a time of quiet. A three-to-
five-minute mind-clearing meditation at any time,
day or night, offers surprisingly deep refreshment to
our spirits. If our lives allow little time for solitude,
we can make full use of even a brief interval to nurture our deeper selves.

Today, a time of solitude revives my spirit.

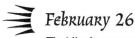 *February 26*

*That I'm homosexual seems like a sure thing —
I've associated with myself for nearly forty years.*

MUTSUO TAKAHASHI

We can trust our own feelings, memories, dreams, and experiences to tell us who we are, what we value most, and what we desire in our lives. Though others may ask useful questions or make observations that prompt us to question our denials and to look more deeply within, they don't necessarily have the answers we're seeking. Often, others have needs and agendas of their own that subtly influence how they define us. Books, families, teachers, well-meaning friends, and even trusted counselors are less well informed about us than our own inner guidance is.

Sometimes our question is as fundamental as "Am I gay?" or "Am I having a problem with addiction?" More often, our questions are about smaller issues, yet our serenity seems to depend on finding the answers right now. It is then that we need to look within, explore our own hearts, and acknowledge the truth we find there.

Today, the answers to my questions lie within me.

February 27

and I have been branded
dyke, bitch, manhater,
diseased. *For some*
this means I'm crazy.
For others I don't exist.

JANET AALFS

As lesbian, gay, bisexual, or transgender people,
we've often been left out or defined through negative stereotypes. When we've expressed long-
ignored needs and feelings or when we've given
vent to anger and frustration, some have called
us crazy.

There's nothing crazy about wanting to be included as members of the human family, to have
our needs and visions respected. Our desire to use
our creative energies and bring our ideas to fruition
comes from a part of us that's sane and whole—the
opposite of "crazy."

We must learn to love and trust ourselves unconditionally. Our fundamental desires are healthy
ones. They are worthy of our acknowledgment and
support. As we come to recognize and validate our
own and one another's gifts, desires, and dreams,
we are nurturing the wholeness from which visions
and acts of self-empowerment spring.

Today, I trust my desire for wholeness and health.

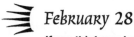

February 28

If you think you know what you will find,
Then you will find nothing.

LAWRENCE KUSHNER

Lesbians, gay men, and bisexual or transgender people are not automatically exempt from the temptation to prejudge. Perhaps we assume that we know the truth about those who define themselves differently from us; perhaps we make generalizations about the groups of which we ourselves are a part; or perhaps we make hasty, broad statements that fail to acknowledge our complexity and individual differences. Sometimes it's easier to agree with what we perceive as the "party line" than to stay open to the unknown.

If we refuse to be governed by our own prejudices, we may find friends where we never expected to. If we refuse to be controlled by our fear of unknown experiences, we will find the world a far richer place and our own souls more alive with possibility.

Today, I keep an open mind about the
people, places, and things I don't know yet.

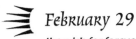 *FebRuary 29*

the wish for forever
for more often
for more

CHERYL CLARKE

Many of us postponed coming out as lesbian, gay, bisexual, or transgender as we struggled with fear or prejudice, both our own and that of others. Now that we're out, we may be trying to make up for lost time.

We may want to rush through the process of getting to know another person, unrealistically expecting guarantees of permanence soon after we meet. We may try to numb feelings of insecurity or fear by instantly bringing sex into a relationship. We may cling to another person as to a life raft, hoping we'll never again have to feel unloved or lonely.

Mutual understanding and commitment evolve through a process of communication and growth over time. Relationships are not drugs or magic; they don't happen instantly and they don't offer guarantees. We can allow ourselves time to evaluate the potential for a lasting relationship as we continue to nurture ourselves and to develop as individuals. The more we take mature responsibility for our own happiness, the more we bring to our relationships with others.

Today, I'm willing to take time for the
process of relationships.

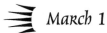

March 1

When things are going great, so well you feel almost on a nonalcoholic high—look out!

Living Sober

Liberating processes such as coming out or entering recovery may fill us with elation. We may have a sense of hope and freedom, in sharp contrast to former feelings of depression or confusion. We're sitting on top of the world, ready to shout out the story of our dramatic transformation to whoever will listen.

Joy is a wonderful and necessary part of life. But we would be wise to pay attention to feelings of intense elation that can throw us off balance or trigger a relapse. To maintain our equilibrium, we can keep taking actions that have helped us stay on an even keel so far: staying in close touch with trusted friends or sponsors, participating in community events or meetings, and continuing to feed body and soul with proper nourishment, exercise, and spiritual practice. Above all, we can cultivate a healthy sense of humor about ourselves and the dramas in our lives.

Today, I stay with practices
that help me keep my balance.

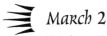 ## March 2

Coming out, I managed. Staying out *is hard.*
ALLAN GURGANUS

There are moments of vision and experience that transform our lives. Our first awareness of ourselves as lesbian, gay, bisexual, or transgender may be one of these moments. For those in recovery, our first Twelve Step meeting is often such a moment. Peak experiences can give us the inspiration and courage we need for the work that follows. But after a time of transforming vision, we may find ourselves plunged into a new reality that makes many demands on us. Once the first excitement has passed, we may balk at the thought of what lies ahead.

The strengthening of our identity, values, and commitments occurs over and over again, through small daily acts and affirmations, through challenges met and conflicts weathered and resolved. Being ourselves is something we work at, one day at a time. We don't have to do it alone. Our communities—including our chosen families of friends and loved ones, peers and sponsors in recovery, and spiritual and psychological counselors—are in our lives to support us as we continue on our journeys.

Today, I take another step that affirms
my identity and chosen path.

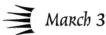 ## March 3

As far as my life is concerned, poetry has saved me again and again.

MURIEL RUKEYSER

Reading and writing are among the tools many of us find most powerful in our process of personal transformation. For those who struggle with issues of identity or who are recovering from the isolation and denial of addiction, both reading and writing offer inspiration and validation.

It is rare that we turn to such media as newspapers, television, or the products of popular culture for reflections of our real selves, our struggles, and our celebrations. But we do find lives like our own represented in a wealth of literature, whether of liberation or recovery, whose purpose is to tell the truth and to tell it in memorable language.

It's not surprising that so many of us—whether or not we are professional writers—find healing expression in creating poems, stories, and plays, keeping journals, or making written inventories as part of the Twelve Step recovery process. We can write truthfully from our deep places. Whether or not we wish to share our writing with others, we can use it as part of our process of healing and growth.

Today, I use reading and writing
as ways to connect to the truth within me.

 ## March 4

My next lover will have something she's impassioned about and obsessed with besides me.

BECKY BIRTHA

How tempting it is to let affection and caring for another person become obsessive. Immersion in another person's life helps us forget that we have our own visions to follow, our own responsibilities and dreams. Instead of going through the discomfort that pursuing separate needs or goals evokes in us, we may deny their importance, content to bask in our partner's light. In time, we may grow bored or resentful. When love began, we were quick to set our needs aside; now we may find it difficult to re-assert them.

By maintaining healthy boundaries between ourselves and those we love, we have more to offer one another, more delight and vitality in coming together, than when we are merged and codependent. Equal partnerships require that we respect the ways that we are different and separate from one another. Nurturing ourselves appropriately makes us more generous as we nurture and receive nurturing from those we love.

Today, I strengthen all my relationships by remaining true to myself.

March 5

From five hundred miles away
jealousy can hear
the crumpling of a pillow
beneath two heads.

NAOMI REPLANSKY

When the green-eyed monster, jealousy, takes up
residence in our heads, everything we used to know
about ourselves shrinks and disappears. Suddenly,
our lives are all about lack. We don't have enough
affection; we don't have enough money. We've
missed out on the lover, the grant, the promotion,
the inheritance. Our bodies, homes, wardrobes,
work—all that we have is inadequate compared
with what others have, with what *they* have stolen
from us!

In this turbulent and painful state of mind, we
can sometimes step back and see how absurd our
claims to superiority or inferiority are. Comparing
ourselves unfavorably with others, insisting that
we've missed out on what matters, casts a pall over
our lives and disempowers us, as any obsession
will. If we're suffering from jealousy, it's time to
take a deep breath and to pray for abundance and
fulfillment in the lives of those we envy. Whether
our prayers are open-hearted or begin grudgingly,
in time generosity will flow from us again, toward
ourselves and others.

Today, I am grateful for abundance
in my own and others' lives.

 ## March 6

However briefly, I had known what it was to have my desire returned, and it spoiled me for mere friendship. I wanted more. . . . But he had made up his mind. He was never unkind about it, but he made it clear that the experiment would not be repeated.

MICHAEL NAVA

Others close to us may define themselves in terms different from those we've embraced, or our own desires and timetables may not be in sync with theirs. It's not unusual for someone whose love we crave to be unable to respond to us in kind, or for someone we hoped would join us on our sober path to be unwilling to face an addiction. How are we to deal with such disappointments?

We must allow others the same freedom of choice, the same time for growth and transformation, that we ourselves require. Denying what we've heard someone tell us about herself or himself or blaming or attacking someone whose will conflicts with ours only perpetuates pain. Rather than cultivate disappointment, we can let go of unrealistic expectations. When we've acknowledged and accepted our sense of disappointment and loss, we can move forward. We can become open to the abundance and variety of new experiences about to enter our lives.

Today, I survive disappointment and stay open to new experiences.

 *March 7*

Would I be as strong as she had been, as hungry for love, as desperate, determined, and ashamed?

DOROTHY ALLISON

Who were our parents and what were their dreams and desires? How have our families influenced who we are? As people with lesbian, gay, bisexual, or transgender identities, many of us have defined ourselves differently from the way our family members have. This is also true of some who are recovering from addictions. We may experience our families as having rejected us; we in turn may have rejected them.

Over time, as we assume responsibility for our adult actions and take steps to fulfill our own dreams, we may begin to see family members differently. Like us, they have been shaped by circumstances not entirely of their own making. Like us, they may have tried to do their best. Understanding the context for their limitations, we may see them with greater compassion. Anger and alienation may lessen and forgiveness may begin to be possible. Whatever the shortcomings of our families, we have the freedom to make choices that nurture our adult selves.

Today, I see myself and others as whole human beings. I forgive them, and I forgive myself.

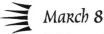 *March 8*

Religion and art spring from the same root and are close kin. Economics and art are strangers.

WILLA CATHER

As adults, we have become more practical about meeting our economic needs and responsibilities. Perhaps we've gone so far in the process of learning to be fiscally responsible that we've become greedy or cynical. Some of us may have forgotten that there are things more sacred than monetary success.

Creativity, play, love, connection to a Higher Power, joy—all of these are among our needs. They are as important to our spirits as food and shelter are to our physical survival. If we've given up on our creative side because "it doesn't pay" or because we're "not good enough to succeed," we may be denying the spirit within us the nourishment it yearns for. We must determine what success means to each of us; we need not be limited by others' definitions or goals. Creative expression is its own reward. It is the voice of our soul.

Today, I express my creativity in something I do, simply for its own sake.

 *March 9*

This body, which appears so fragile, is none-theless more durable than my virtuous resolutions, perhaps even more durable than my soul.

MARGUERITE YOURCENAR

With the help of our bodies, which always speak to us eloquently and truthfully, we've come to understand our true identities. We've survived living in a society that has not yet given full acceptance to those with lesbian, gay, bisexual, or transgender identities. Many of us have responded to our bodies' pleas for healing and are living in recovery, learning to nourish ourselves in new ways.

Our spirit communicates with us through our bodies. It's up to us to listen. If we're numbing ourselves with food or chemical substances; if we're risking illness through ignoring our bodies' need for rest, exercise, and appropriate nourishment; if we're out of touch with our capacity for sensuality and sexuality; if we're mistreating our bodies through overwork, stress, violence, or abuse, then the body will voice its protest. Awareness and love for our bodies are necessary if we're to keep our connection to Spirit clear and open.

Today, I pay loving attention to my body. I have the willingness to meet its needs.

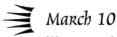

March 10

*We gay people have far more allies than we tend
to realize; we must risk asking for their support.*

JOYCE MURDOCH

We need not live exclusively in lesbian, gay, bisexual, or transgender environments. There is support for us in the larger community as well, if we are willing to seek it. We may prefer surrounding ourselves with people whose identities, needs, and concerns are closest to our own. Are we choosing freely or simply masking our fears? Our need for the protection and affirmation of separate organizations and environments varies, depending on such things as what sort of work we do, how tolerant and open the larger communities we live in are, and where we are in exploring the process of coming out.

We no longer need to depend on bars, nightclubs, and acting-out environments to meet others like us. The rich resources of community centers, bookstores, Twelve Step meetings, spiritual groups, or other organizations devoted to the needs of lesbian, gay, bisexual, and transgender people are gifts. And it's a gift when we can also participate openly in the larger community, where the welcome for our presence and participation is growing.

*Wherever I am today, I welcome others
and am open to being welcomed in return.*

March 11

I think of the wonderful laughter of a room full of women, the excited talking. The joy. Or the almost blistering crackle of energy in a room full of women when one is singing or reading her work to the others. Every word counts.

SUSAN GRIFFIN

As lesbian, gay, bisexual, and transgender people, we need access to the knowledge of others like us— of one another's true stories, losses and survival, grief and celebration, courage, enormous talents, and capacity for feeling and expression. Now is the time to encourage and to listen well. We must cherish each other's memories, discoveries, scientific and historical research, artistic expression, and healing rituals.

We can listen actively, open to recognizing feelings and experiences like our own. As wholehearted listeners, we receive the gift of identification with others; we learn that we are not alone. Recovery, too, shows us that our lives can be illuminated and healed through the simple process of listening, as others like ourselves share openly their experience, strength, and hope.

Every word counts.

Today, I listen with all my attention.

 *March 12*

*What would happen if one woman
told the truth about her life?
    The world would split open.*

MURIEL RUKEYSER

As lesbian, gay, bisexual, and transgender people,
we tend to be careful about what we reveal of our
true selves—a habit based on long experience of
navigating territories we suspect are hostile.

   We must take care not to let our hiding go too
far, not to separate ourselves from the support of
others, not to isolate ourselves with our secrets. We
must take care not to assume that there is nowhere
we are safe to reveal our identities and concerns.
We must beware of perpetuating silence, depriving
others as well as ourselves of the truth.

   Twelve Step programs are among the places
where it's essential to be willing to share ourselves
honestly. We feel the exhilaration of freedom when
we let go of long-held secrets and discover that others, far from being critical and rejecting, understand
and identify with us. Recovery, our own and that of
others, depends on honesty.

Today, I share with all my honesty.

 *March 13*

I believe it is possible for all of us, at any age, to learn to see beneath the surface into the more real and rewarding parts of the people we meet. I think of that now as looking into others' souls.

RAYMOND BERGER

In our process of maturing as gay, lesbian, trans-gender, and bisexual people, we're learning to see and appreciate ourselves and others as whole human beings. We're not limited by superficial standards of attractiveness imposed by the larger culture. Attractiveness is in our attitudes. When we esteem and enjoy ourselves, others are attracted to our positiveness. In turn, we're capable of great depth and discernment, learning to see the beauty of each person's unique energy and experience. We're drawn to warmth, sincerity, and originality. We appreciate the spirit that moves people and makes them who they are.

Our appreciation of every kind of beauty goes hand in hand with our acceptance and love of ourselves.

Today, I see beyond the surface.
I know and appreciate my own and others' beauty.

March 14

> *In the dark of the night and wild night surf roaring
> I realize how furious I've been . . . spluttering inco-
> herent rage at all the silence, all the denial, all the
> women called crazy, all the years lost, all the chil-
> dren, all the free perpetrators, all of them, the rage
> relentless as the pounding ocean, keening and
> howling and beating at the screens of this cottage.
> I feel afire, driven, ran up the road in the night and
> back.*

ANNA RICHARDSON

Some of us are seeking healing from incest, rape, abuse, or violence. We needn't numb painful memories with addictive substances or behaviors. Instead, there are avenues of healing expression open to us.

Anger is likely to be one of our responses to memories of traumatic experience and to the silence and denial that may have prevented us from acknowledging the impact of such an experience on our lives. Anger can be a positive, cleansing force, driving out falsehood, depression, and despair. We needn't fear the power of anger, our own or that of others. When we've allowed the storm to sweep through us and leave, we sense that we are growing strong enough to weather all we know to be true.

Today, I'm grateful for cleansing anger.

 ## March 15

Living as a negative entity in a positive world is the predicament of the gay man, lesbian, or bisexual who does not accept himself or herself and of the individual who does not accept that he or she has a chemical or behavioral dependency. Living like this is living in a nightmare.

KATHRYN AND SHEPPARD KOMINARS

In the past, denial may have played a significant role in our lives. There may be denials that continue to lock us into suffering today.

We need to look honestly at our lives, asking ourselves whether or not denial is a part of our experience. Perhaps we are still disowning the truth and dignity of our identities, needs, and desires as lesbian, gay, bisexual, or transgender people. Some of us may still rely on addictive substances or behaviors for consolation or uplift. We may have rationalized our neglect of meaningful relationships, work, or creative or spiritual expression. We may be putting up with victimhood or depression.

Perhaps, up to now, we've found the familiarity of the status quo comforting in its way, less threatening than a change we imagine would turn our world around. Now is the time to confront our denials, to stop settling for less than complete aliveness.

Today, I confront my old denials with honesty. I begin to accept and live the truth.

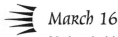

March 16

Made a decision to turn our will and our lives over to the care of God as we understood Him.

Step Three of the
Twelve Steps of Alcoholics Anonymous

Some of us have old, uncomfortable associations with the word "God"; we may even find "Higher Power" difficult to use. We may think Step Three suggests that we stop taking responsibility for our lives.

Step Three doesn't propose that we accept anyone else's concept of a Higher Power or that we live passively. Lesbian, gay, bisexual, or transgender people who are leery of religious concepts may still agree that we have something within that inspires us. We may refer to it as "spiritual energy," "the life force," or "our best self." We sense that when we take actions such as coming out or acknowledging an addiction, we're deciding to honor the truth of our own beings. We're given no guarantees concerning outcomes, but something in us refuses to continue denying our truth. We take a risk. We make a decision. We step into the unknown, with what we might be willing to call faith.

Today, I let my best self guide my actions.
I accept that I'm not in control of outcomes.

 ## March 17

Never doubt that a small group of committed people can change the world.

MARGARET MEAD

We are on a path of change. None of us has become perfect, but we have made significant progress. We are less the victims of old obsessions and compulsions. We're no longer weighed down by such low self-esteem. We have begun connecting to ourselves and our Higher Power. We've made worthy commitments. We're learning to trust ourselves.

Today, we are freer to rock the boat. We do not have to accept the status quo, either in our own lives or in the community and world around us. We can begin to engage in the revolutionary act of becoming fully ourselves, living our values, accepting our own power to help in the creation of understanding, love, peace, light, and brotherhood and sisterhood in the world. We can cooperate with others who share our ideals.

There is hope for the world as long as each one of us knows that we're capable of continuing to grow and change.

Today, I help to create positive change in myself and in my world.

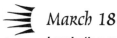

March 18

I am both a conservative and a radical; I would conserve what is valuable but willingly change what requires changing.

ERIC MAISEL

We have the responsibility not to make promises lightly or thoughtlessly; the commitments we make to ourselves and others are important. But consistency doesn't mean we're never allowed to change our thinking or our lives.

As we plan our day, let's remind ourselves of our primary purpose, planning to keep the promises and commitments we've made. Let's also examine things we're doing that are a source of discomfort and consider departing from a habit or personal tradition that no longer fits us. Our sense of ourselves can be independent and fluid enough to support our growth. We can open our minds about what is possible for us to be and do, and we can bring our lives into truer alignment with our deep understanding of ourselves. Let's plan that as new situations arise, we will make any new commitments with care, first considering our ability and willingness to keep them. We need not be limited by local ideas and customs, by roles that have been imposed by the culture, or by others' expectations of how we ought to express our identity.

Today, I expand my sense of who I am and can be.

March 19

I like to work. If I'm in a circumstance where I'm not doing any work, then I do something else like it. . . . I look for mushrooms, or I look at the situation in which I find myself. . . . If I'm standing in line in the supermarket, which is another kind of solitude, I ask, how can I spend my time there without just being impatient? And the way to do it is by paying attention to the environment.

JOHN CAGE

Truly paying attention to what is in front of us can be a meditation. It is a way of being alive in the moment and appreciating reality, instead of having an attitude of impatience or boredom. If we engage actively with what we see and hear—noticing what *is*, not just our judgments about it—we will find the unexpected.

When we have tasks to perform, we can give them our whole attention, instead of simply hurrying to finish. Cooking for ourselves, caring for a sick friend, and even paying our bills needn't be tedious experiences if we don't resist them. When we cook, for example, we can take time to appreciate the color, texture, smell, and taste of the food we're preparing. We can give thanks for the gift of nourishment and eat with gratefulness. Whatever we are engaged in doing, we can live each moment as if it were created for us, meant to allow us to pause and be refreshed.

Today, I bring my full attention to whatever I do.

 ## March 20

*What I learned at Denis' memorial service yester-
day was that people love you and remember you
for being yourself, not for concealing and easing
but for expressing. . . . Defects of character don't
matter that much either—what matters is to give
yourself to the world, to express yourself.*

ANNA RICHARDSON

The gay, lesbian, bisexual, and transgender community has witnessed many deaths, so many that it
sometimes seems as if there could never be time to
complete all of our grieving. Yet, whenever one of
our community has left this life, we've been shown
how we need to use the gift of time we've been
given. The generosity of the dying has been to teach
us to be our real selves. Being with them reminds us
that love and truthfulness can go together: the
dying have no time or use for pretense. As we think
about those we've been privileged to know, we're
aware of their range of feelings, their thorny sides,
and their human limitations. We loved and looked
up to them, not *in spite of* their failings, but in part
because they allowed us to know them as they were.

Today, I dare to be myself.

 Maʀch 21

*For many people the most difficult thing in the
world is to learn to mind their own business.*

J. KRISHNAMURTI

Perhaps we think we know the perfect medical alternative or nutritional plan for a sick friend, have
the name of a counselor who could help the couple
whose relationship is in trouble, or know someone
in desperate need of Twelve Step recovery. We have
difficulties of our own, but working to resolve them
seems somehow less pressing than the problems of
our friends and loved ones.

It's human to want to help others, but we may
be evading our own problems when we insist on
having the answers for others. When people near
us are in crisis, it is best to offer advice only when
asked. Often, all that's needed is a listening ear.
When we're tempted to rescue others, we should
ask ourselves whether we are helping or simply in-
terfering. We ourselves don't want others to try to
fix us. We appreciate simply being heard and validated. Instead of urging our solutions on others,
we can listen with respect and understanding. It is
a gift.

*Today, I listen and support.
I don't give unwanted advice.*

March 22

*The hard rain and wind
are ways the cloud has
to take care of us.*

RUMI

It's the nature of human life to keep changing.
Sometimes, instead of joy, life seems to bring only
problems. At times we may feel overwhelmed with
frustration and disappointment. As a problem is
resolved, it explodes with myriad seeds of new
ones. The more we embrace life, the more we risk.
We can no longer withdraw into isolation or retreat
from involvement with other people and life for
more than a brief time. That option is no longer
open to us. Whether through coming out or entering recovery—both, for many of us—we've taken an
irrevocable step into a life touched by the lives of
others. We are blessed to experience both joy and
sadness as part of this life. Our griefs, instead of di-
minishing us, can expand our hearts with compassion for others.

*Today, grief teaches me to be more compassionate
and loving.*

 ## March 23

It just isn't true that gay people are lonelier than ungay people (or whatever the opposite of gay is), and I'm in a position to know.

NED ROREM

The old myths about our lives no longer need to determine how we think of ourselves or how we're seen by others. There's so much evidence that contradicts negative images of lesbian, gay, bisexual, and transgender people. These are not the gloomy days when the only places where we knew we could find one another evoked danger and low self-esteem. We have large, supportive communities in which many of us work cooperatively for common causes. There are numerous organizations that bring us together for support, activism, or fun, and there are thriving Twelve Step programs that meet our needs for healing and fellowship. We know where to find friends and how to reach out to one another, if that is what we want. Whether or not we are in primary loving relationships, we do not have to live our lives in loneliness. It's a choice.

Today, I make a choice to be alone or with others.

 *March 24*

The god in him had cried out to the god in me.

MARY RENAULT

There are times when we seem to be looking directly into the depths of another person's soul. We associate these moments of deep communication and closeness—seeming oneness—with sexual intimacy, but in fact they can occur in a friendship or in any kind of relationship that permits us to come together in a profound experience of sharing. At such privileged moments, we sense that our human love is both a part and an expression of something larger. We sense that we are channels for a loving energy that fuels the universe.

We can't always have peak experiences. But we can see the divine in others, if we look for it. We can treat as sacred all the ways that our lives touch other lives. We can share in a way that allows others to begin to see into our souls.

Today, all my relationships are part of my relationship with a Higher Power.

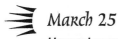 ## Μarch 25

*I learned a word could hush
A room.*

JANET AALFS

As lesbian, gay, bisexual, or transgender people, we know the power of words to destroy or heal. Others may have used words to stereotype or insult us. We ourselves may have used words as weapons, against ourselves or against others. When we took the leap of defining ourselves, some may have experienced our words as blows.

Our movements of liberation have been movements shaped in large part by words. Our activists have included writers; our poets have been among our most eloquent spokespeople. They have expressed our instinctive awareness that the language we use has the power to create new visions of ourselves.

We can treat language with respect and conscious care, using it to represent our experience, strength, and hope accurately and to sow seeds of understanding and compassion.

*Today, I consciously choose words to express
my love and respect for myself.*

March 26

Re-examine all you have been told at school or church or in any book, dismiss whatever insults your own soul, and your very flesh shall be a great poem.

WALT WHITMAN

We've come too far, taken too great a leap into the void, to be willing to let others define our experience for us. We recognize the truth when we encounter it. We shiver, weep, laugh, or simply sit in silent gratitude. When a gay, lesbian, bisexual, or transgender artist portrays the truth of his or her experience, we recognize and identify with it. When someone speaking at a recovery meeting shares honestly, our souls respond.

A sense of community is one of our greatest resources. It's essential for us to find and create situations where we can hear and identify with others like ourselves as they bear witness to their experience, strength, and hope. Without such witnessing, without identification, we are alone again, struggling in isolation and shame with our old beliefs about ourselves and our experience.

We need to hear, over and over, how others' lives resemble our own.

Today, I am committed to maintaining a relationship with a community in which I can identify with others.

March 27

Brother, we must converse somehow.

ELEANOR ROSS TAYLOR

Too much is at stake for us to believe the old idea that lesbians, gay men, bisexuals, and transgender people are too different to appreciate one another or work together. Some of us are living and dying with AIDS or breast cancer without adequate community understanding or support. Some of us are victims of violence or abuse. Some of us are young people at risk of suicide or addiction. What would happen if we let go of any ideas of competition, scarcity, or apathy that divide us?

Such divisions come from a fear that our needs will not be met. But the more generous we are to one another, the more we ourselves are nourished and strengthened by connection. We have a wealth of experience, courage, and sensitivity to offer one another. Each loving community can continue to grow if we let down the barriers between us.

Today, I expand my sense of family. I lovingly affirm my connection to my sisters and brothers.

March 28

*Homosexuality should not only be homosexual
but also homoerotic.*

MUTSUO TAKAHASHI

Perhaps we've struggled so hard with questions of
identity or recovery, illness, politics, reinventing the
family, making ourselves visible in the workplace
and the community, aging, and more, that we've let
the erotic fade in importance in our lives. Perhaps
we've been too busy just surviving. Perhaps we're in
a long-term partnership in which we've forgotten to
make time for the erotic. Perhaps we believe that we
can't honor our erotic nature if we're single.

Our sensual side springs from the same life energy as our spiritual side. It is one of the ways to express our love for others, ourselves, and our Higher
Power. If it is to flourish, we must make time for it,
cultivate it, celebrate it. It's a medium of communication, pleasure, nourishment, fantasy, and play.
Honoring it may include periods of celibacy as well
as activity. It requires sensitivity to our own and a
partner's differing needs. And always, it requires
that we practice safe sex. Self-esteem and mutual
respect can be an integral part of our erotic lives.

*Today, I honor my sensuality and sexuality
in ways that meet my present needs.*

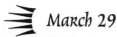

March 29

Nothing can reckon with you, if you can reckon with yourself.

JIM EVERHARD

We are blessed to know who we are. Each of us may have questioned our identity for a time. But our early intuitions, our ongoing experiences of strong feelings, and the fundamental honesty that makes denial impossible to maintain, even in the face of others' disapproval or rejection, have re-inforced the clarity we feel. Having defined our-selves, we can't be intimidated by any threat of being unmasked or excluded by others. There is strength and security in knowing and naming our-selves. This is true not only with regard to sexual identity, but in other areas of our lives as well. For many of us, the admission of powerlessness over an addictive substance or behavior has empowered us to live in the truth of recovery.

Only we ourselves can say with authority what is or is not part of what defines us. Claiming the various aspects of our own complex, unique iden-tity frees and empowers us.

Today, I am strong, proud, and free as I claim my own identity.

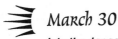

March 30

Into the dangerous world I leapt.

WILLIAM BLAKE

Life is full of risks. We may be tempted to maintain the status quo in areas of our lives where we've achieved some kind of stability, even though our deep needs aren't being fulfilled. We may be reluctant to reach out to new friends or potential loves if we are grieving a loss or hurt. We may not want to take on the risk of changing jobs, the expense of furthering our education, or the hard work of pursuing recovery or therapy.

There are no guarantees that we'll like the new experiences for which we've exchanged our old ones. We may be loath to change routines that are familiar and comforting. We are not lazy. More likely, we're feeling frightened or inadequate. Many courageous people have experienced the hesitation we're experiencing. Courage is not the absence of fear; it is having the willingness to take action in spite of fear.

Today, I'm willing to risk doing something differently.

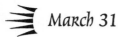 **March 31**

*you were a witness
who knew she would not be believed.*

GAIL HANLON

At times we're more conscious than usual of the ways that lesbian, gay, bisexual, and transgender people are marginalized in our society. A colleague's assumption that we're heterosexual, a denial of benefits for a domestic partner, or an experience of harassment can leave us with a deep sense of injustice.

Instead of simply marshaling our old defenses of resentment or fear, we can cultivate responses that come from a sense of wholeness and high self-esteem. We needn't participate in or internalize definitions that denigrate our sexuality. Rather than always taking a reactive position, we can sometimes begin to take the lead in our relationships with other people and institutions. We can affirm to ourselves and others our boundaries, needs, and traditions. We can be assertive without being defensive.

Today, I don't simply react to others. I'm willing to say who I am and what I need. I'm willing at times to lead.

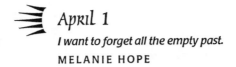

April 1

I want to forget all the empty past.

MELANIE HOPE

Memories can delight us or pain us as we look back at the past. The process in Step Four of making "a searching and fearless moral inventory of ourselves" is the beginning of a way to look at our histories honestly and constructively.

As we begin to see and acknowledge the patterns we've repeated, the impact of our actions on others, and the consequences to ourselves, we don't have to punish ourselves with regrets about the past or fears about the future. We can recognize where we've come from, what gifts we've been blessed with, and what areas of denial or conflict we wish to heal. Perhaps it's time to face an addictive substance or behavior that stands between us and our connection to a Higher Power. Perhaps we are ready to take another step in the unfolding of lesbian, gay, bisexual, or transgender identity. Taking an inventory of the past can help us commit to the process of change.

Today, I accept my entire past. I see myself with compassion.

April 2

We are everywhere.

Message on signs held by lesbian and gay marchers

Sometimes we think our lives would be easier or fuller if only we lived somewhere else. Some of us want to move farther away from our biological families or from people with whom we grew up, convinced that we can't be our true selves close to home. Some want to escape to communities where there are higher concentrations of people who identify themselves as we do.

We need to look searchingly at our dissatisfaction with where we are. While there's no denying that some communities and institutions are more aware and tolerant of the gay, lesbian, bisexual, or transgender people in their midst, there's no geographic cure for issues whose answers lie within us. Our attitudes are more important than our physical environment. When we're comfortable with ourselves, we can be comfortable in most places. Wherever we live or work, we will find others who accept us as we are.

Today, I see opportunities in my environment and community for acceptance and fulfillment.

April 3

All things ceased; I went out from myself.

JOHN OF THE CROSS

Meditative practice need not be complicated or difficult. It can be a place we go within ourselves that offers relief, peace, aliveness, beauty, and joy. We can go there without a sense of effort or boredom.

We can choose which form of meditation to practice. As with anything else in life, our choice can grow out of experience and understanding of ourselves and our needs. One form of meditation is to greet the presence of Spirit in everything around us and within us. Whether or not we have a name for it, we acknowledge the energy that sustains all life. The sensation of our own breathing, the sounds around us, the people whose lives touch ours—all are expressions of Spirit, all are interconnected. With each breath, each thought, we affirm and deepen our awareness of our Higher Power, however we choose to name it.

Today, I improve my conscious contact with my Higher Power through meditation.

April 4

It is good to see the golden bees climb into the purple crocus bells. It is also good to see the gray rats at the dump pounce on the garbage I bring there, see them scurry off with old potato skins for their children. Both are spring, both are life.

ROBERT FRANCIS

In spring, we are especially aware of life's energy and self-renewal. Perhaps we think of nature's beauty as serene or majestic, forgetting the parts of nature that are hungry, fierce, intent on survival.

We, too, are part of nature, and we share with other creatures the need for renewal. Some of our need for renewal is physical: moving our bodies, getting enough exercise to stay healthy, eating food that nourishes us. Some of our need for renewal is mental and spiritual. We need the stimulation of other people and ideas and the centering that comes from maintaining a healthy ongoing relationship with a Higher Power.

We can take an inventory of our physical, mental, and spiritual needs, asking ourselves which hungers are being satisfied and which are being left unfed. We can seek ways to renew our flow of energy and our appetite for life.

Today, I take an action that contributes to my self-renewal.

April 5

What we're asking for are equal rites.

KATHLEEN BOATWRIGHT

Some of us continue to find the basis of our beliefs and the context of our spiritual expression in the religion we were taught to follow as children. Others, some of whom may have awakened to spiritual needs in a Twelve Step program, have begun new explorations of spiritual practices and institutions. Even those of us who have embraced atheism experience the desire at times for rituals to mark significant passages in our lives and to connect us with our communities.

Many lesbian, gay, bisexual, and transgender people have been ingenious at creating unique rituals that express and sanctify our relationships with ourselves, each other, and life's mysteries: rituals of healing, commitment, the passage from life to death, or the celebration of anniversaries and significant accomplishments. Others have spoken out as members of churches and synagogues, calling for affirmation and inclusion in observances, rites of passage, and celebrations to which all of us are entitled.

Today, I celebrate my sexuality as a blessing.

April 6

Doubt indulged soon becomes doubt realized.

FRANCES HAVERGAL

There is no faith without moments of doubt and deep discouragement. We may wonder whether we have chosen the right path, whether we have the courage needed to fulfill our dreams, or whether others in our lives can find the inner guidance we want for them. Perhaps we feel overwhelmed by difficulties and disappointments. We wonder what sort of Higher Power would burden us with more than we can handle.

At such times, instead of giving ourselves over to doubt or despair, we can expand our faith and envision a Higher Power that is larger than the limitations of our understanding and faith. We can envision infinite love and compassion, infinite wisdom, infinite patience and power to heal. As we affirm these qualities in our Higher Power, our own compassion, wisdom, patience, and gift for healing are fed and strengthened.

Today, I make my Higher Power larger than anything I have so far imagined.

April 7

*I remember . . . the feeling of that soft spot
just north-east of the corner of your mouth
against my lips.*

ELEANOR ROOSEVELT
In a letter to Lorena Hickok

When lesbian, gay, bisexual, or transgender documents have come to light, they've often been ignored, sanitized, or suppressed. This is especially true about lives of people whose accomplishments we celebrate. Despite clear evidence, some historians, biographers, journalists, and critics have attempted to "save" reputations, protesting that it is "immoral" or "unthinkable" to suspect certain people of nonheterosexual experience. Our intuition and the work of researchers dedicated to truth tell us that nonconforming sexualities are less rare than we're asked to believe.

Denial of truths so obvious they're like the proverbial "elephant in the living room" is still a part of our culture. Within our communities, we can be part of the solution by acknowledging the importance of one another's contributions and by not denying such widespread problems among us as addiction or abuse. We don't have to settle for anything less than the truth of who we are, have been, and can be.

Today, I embrace the truth.

April 8

In order to keep myself in my marriage and in the straight white way of doing things, I had to keep myself sedated. Heavily. Smoking pot and drinking until the center as well as the edges of my life became fuzzy.

BLAKE C. AARENS

Substance abuse has enabled many of us to stay in socially sanctioned roles that were not what we really wanted. Heterosexual marriages, "passing," or doing whatever we thought was necessary to make ourselves acceptable required that we numb ourselves and our deep desires. Some of us knew what these desires were; others had disconnected from our real selves at an early age and took years to achieve clarity.

Naming ourselves lesbian, gay, bisexual, or transgender, letting go of unwanted roles and liberating our sexuality, has not guaranteed us freedom from addictive habits. Drugs, in many parts of our community, are intimately linked with sexual experience and expression. For many, "going out" or "going dancing" are euphemisms for seeking the combined experience of sex and drugs. Awareness that chemical dependency is a serious problem within our community is a necessary first step toward truly liberating our sexuality.

Today, I look honestly at the role of addiction in my sexual life.

April 9

To try to fill your emptiness with meaning from outside yourself is like pouring water into the ocean to make it wet.

MEL ASH

Some of us look for solutions to our difficulties by searching for a teacher or system of belief that has the answers. We may place our faith in one discipline and then another, hoping someone or something can liberate us. The answers, if we're willing to look deeply enough, often lie within us.

In time, any spiritual path brings us to a point at which we can't avoid ourselves any longer. Perhaps we have yet to accept our sexuality or are facing some obstacle to serenity—a crippling fear, a resentment, or an unacknowledged addiction. Perhaps we have yet to understand the effect of our past and present actions on ourselves and others.

Being *restored* to sanity means returning to the self that we are meant to be: whole, unique individuals, aware of our membership in the human family.

Today, I have the courage to look within.

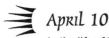

April 10

In the life of the spirit there is no ending that is not a beginning.

HENRIETTA ZOLDE

Many of us have survived deaths of loved ones to breast cancer, AIDS, or other causes. Some of us are living in recovery while family members, former partners, or friends still can't acknowledge the illness of addiction. As we embrace our own lives and commit ourselves to paths of healing and growth, it's not uncommon for us to feel survivor's guilt. Our joy is somehow clouded by our consciousness of what others can't share with us. We're struck by a sense of arbitrariness, wondering how it is that we're alive and recovering while others we love are not.

No one benefits when we cling to a sense of guilt. Guilt is inappropriate in situations where our actions are not the cause of what has or hasn't happened. Our gift to the world is to embrace life wholeheartedly, to let healing and joy fill us, to be fully ourselves. Our lives, not our guilt, are a powerful example and force for good.

Today, I embrace my life and live it fully.

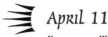 ## April 11

I'm very militant, you know, in a quiet way.

CHRISTOPHER ISHERWOOD

Some of us have been involved in activism, perhaps even assuming positions of leadership in movements for change. Perhaps we've stood supportively on the sidelines or shunned political action altogether. Many would have us believe that theirs is the only right way to bring fairness and justice into the world. But sometimes we may not wish to follow a certain voice or take part in a specific cause. We may feel guilty or inadequate because of the choices we have made. Let's not make ourselves wrong for whoever we are, for whatever contribution we make. Living openly as a bisexual, transgender, lesbian, or gay person is no small achievement. It carries a powerful message of aliveness, self-respect, and clarity. Our happiness and freedom speak eloquently to others like ourselves. We can't underestimate the effect of our example.

*Today, I contribute in my own special way
to justice and freedom.*

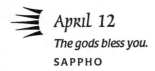

April 12

The gods bless you.

SAPPHO

We have cause for celebration. Though as individuals and as a community we may have suffered losses, let's remember that we are still here and stronger than ever before. Our joys are meant to be spoken, sung, danced, and shared. Celebrations are ways to acknowledge ourselves and one another, give praise and thanks for our accomplishments, strengthen our sense of identity and connection, and reinforce our dedication to our dreams.

We have survived. We have a voice. We have helped to nurture and heal one another, physically and spiritually. We have used our many talents to help make the world saner and more beautiful. We have reinvented the family. We've expanded the known boundaries of love. We've been faithful to our visions.

Today, I have cause to celebrate.

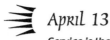 *April 13*

Service is the rent you pay for room on this earth.

SHIRLEY CHISHOLM

None of us could have reached this day entirely on our own. Each of us can look back at moments in our lives when we've been helped or encouraged by another person. A family member, teacher, sponsor, or friend may have offered us mentoring or unconditional love. The words or example of a stranger, a public figure, an artist, or a writer may have afforded us inspiration at just the moment when we needed encouragement.

We can do no less for others as we continue on our journeys. We do not have to take responsibility for others' lives, nor should we disregard our own needs. But there are many ways we can make a difference, each according to our preference. We can offer time and talent to our community, recovery program, or family of choice. We can share our experience, strength, and hope with individuals or groups. We can show up and do some of the work that's necessary to maintain the institutions that have offered so much to us. We can keep it by giving it away.

Today, I express my gratitude through service, freely given.

 **April 14**

Accomplishments have no color.

LEONTYNE PRICE

Having experienced denigrations, exclusions, and hatreds for our identity as lesbian, gay, bisexual, or transgender people, we may have internalized the homophobia that is part of this culture. If we are members of less privileged racial or religious groups, we're likely to have internalized the culture's racism and religious intolerance, as well. Perhaps we find it acceptable to blame or insult those whose gender differs from ours. If we ourselves participate in any form of intolerance, we're helping to perpetuate the very attitudes that have made us "other." Our having been victims of bigotry does not excuse our own intolerance.

It is time to look searchingly and courageously at our fear, hatred, or resentment of other members of the human family. Our own self-esteem increases as we see others whole and worthy of our respect.

Today, I contribute to peace and tolerance through my sense of loving connection with all members of the human family.

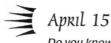 ## April 15

*Do you know what i mean when i say i'm a
human being first and a woman by accident
and a lesbian by preference?*

JILL JOHNSTON

We may speak as if there is only one way to arrive at
an identity, but the truth is more complex. For many
of us, the fact of our gay, lesbian, bisexual, or transgender identity has always been a given. We could
make the decision to suppress or deny it, but we
could not change it. For others, movements of liberation and a climate of increasing tolerance may have
expanded our choices. One example is the decision
some have made to acknowledge increasingly clear
inner guidance and to change gender identities.

The process of transformation differs for each
of us. This is also true for those who embrace recovery as a path of change. Some of us enter recovery after losing everything; others choose recovery
early in the progression of damage that addictions
cause. Some were candidates for addiction from
childhood; others became addicted as adults, perhaps as part of a lifestyle or as an anesthetic for
feelings about sexuality.

Many differences exist among us. No one can
make us feel wrong for our unique path. We ourselves hold the key to naming who we are and how
we got here.

*Today, I respect the uniqueness of my identity
and chosen path.*

April 16

Officer, I was not trying to convert her.

ELEANOR LERMAN

We who have struggled to understand and affirm
our own identities know that we can't impose such
life-changing choices on anyone else. This is true for
lesbian, gay, bisexual, or transgender people and
for those recovering from dependency on addictive
substances or behaviors. People move in the direction that is right for them when they are ready.

Awareness, acceptance, and action are stages of
a highly personal process that occurs over time. We
don't assume that we know what decision or timetable is right for others. We don't try to force our
point of view or to exploit those who are less powerful than we are. We do the most good by simply
being ourselves, keeping our agendas clear as we
share our own experience, strength, and hope
rather than giving unsolicited advice. We respect
the uniqueness of each person's identity and path,
as we do our own.

*Today, I respect others' gift for finding their own truths.
I live my life as I believe; I don't have to make converts.*

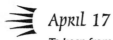 ## April 17

To keep from cryin' I opens my mouths an' laughs.
LANGSTON HUGHES

We often use humor as a way to lighten our burden of grief or anger, to celebrate our unique sensibility, or to express our sense of the ridiculous. Lesbian, gay, bisexual, and transgender writers, performers, and stand-up comedians delight us by helping us identify the wealth of humor in our lives. Sharing comedy reinforces our sense of belonging to a larger community. Laughter itself cleanses and restores us, both physically and spiritually. In recovery, when we share the depths to which addiction has taken us, others at a meeting often laugh with identification and understanding. The laughter of others like ourselves affirms and warms us, giving us courage for whatever work we're facing in our journey of healing and growth. Our sense of humor is a gift. We can cultivate it and remember to draw on it each day.

Today, my heart expands with laughter.

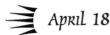 *April 18*

This is the face of an aging woman who looks at me, clear-eyed, from my mirror. This is a face which has known some weathers.

SUSUN WEED

We who identify ourselves as lesbian, gay, bisexual, or transgender have not been exempt from the culture's emphasis on youth and on conventional standards of physical attractiveness, though few of us recognize our real selves in these standardized images. We may focus on diet and exercise regimes to try to stave off the effects of aging or try to change our physical appearance cosmetically or even surgically. We may make jokes about the aging process, subscribing to the belief that our worth lessens as we experience the effects of age.

Maintaining our health is important at any time of our lives. So is recognizing the value of our history of healing and suffering and the gifts that increase, rather than lessen, as we mature. Free from the myth that youth has it all, we can enjoy the company of our peers and share with those who are younger the valuable perspective our experience has bestowed on us. We can acknowledge our own wisdom.

Today, I value the changes time has wrought in me.

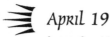 *April 19*

I was about to have my first homosexual experience, but it would be years before I learned to love the homosexuality in myself and in other gay men.

CHARLES SILVERSTEIN

The process of embracing our paths as lesbian, gay, bisexual, or transgender people is one that extends over time as we grow in acceptance, understanding, and love. Self-acceptance is linked to acceptance of others. Including others means more than merely tolerating their presence; it means reaching out, actively attempting to redress the exclusions and injuries of the past. Similarly, accepting ourselves means more than just putting up with who we are; it means rooting out self-hate—acknowledging and letting go of the old belief that we're inferior to others and the secret wish that we were different.

Viewing ourselves and our lives with love is an active process. It means knowing who we are and seeing ourselves with compassion. It means offering full support and enthusiasm to our needs and visions. It means not viewing our desires as separate from those of our Higher Power.

Today, I embrace all that I am with love.

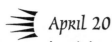 *April 20*

I wanted my hands to be rain for her
to wash away all hurt.

MINNIE BRUCE PRATT

Stories of others' suffering move us to want to help,
to make the world a safer place, to share the healing
we have experienced. We may feel powerless when
we encounter others' suffering in the face of sickness, loss, or violence. We may be tempted to try to
offer a "quick fix" so that we don't have to live
with the anxiety another's pain causes us. We may
feel frustrated that our love and concern can't make
everything better. Or we may withdraw, overwhelmed by problems we know no way of solving.

At such times we can affirm that healing is a
natural tendency and that others have a Higher
Power working in their lives. We can offer unconditional love and moral support. If it's appropriate,
we can share our experience, strength, and hope.
It doesn't help others when we're more active than
they're willing to be in attempting to solve their
problems, or when we neglect our own lives in the
process.

Today, I offer love and understanding
without trying to fix others.

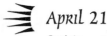 *April 21*

Society . . . as a rule . . . forbids any move which might bring human beings closer to each other.

JACQUES LUSSEYRAN

Perhaps we've learned that we cannot fix others and have resolved to let go of our codependency, keeping the focus on what we can do to heal our own lives. In the process, we may have forgotten that who we are and what we do touches the lives of others. Detachment doesn't mean cutting ourselves off from the rest of the human family. It doesn't mean forgetting that *love* is an active verb.

We can acknowledge the impact of past actions on others and make amends where appropriate. We may have experience, strength, and hope to offer. By accepting the things we cannot change, we can offer compassion and moral support to the sick or to those seeking to transform their lives.

Today, I take responsibility for my actions toward others. I serve others with love and humility.

 **April 22**

*This laboring through what is still undone,
as though, legs bound, we hobbled along the
way, is like the awkward walking of the swan.*

RAINER MARIA RILKE

How close to perfection will we have to come before we're satisfied with our relationships, work,
and creative efforts? Some see every ragged edge,
unsolved problem, or obstacle as evidence of failure. We may criticize ourselves even more harshly
than we do others. We forget that we are works in
progress, that our defects don't keep others from
loving us.

　　None of us has reached perfection. Our
journeys—including bumps and ruts in the road,
including failures that have been our teachers—
have made us more human, more compassionate
toward others. We must view ourselves realistically
and tenderly. To make mistakes is a part of our lives
as they unfold and blossom. We can let go of the
myth of perfection and begin to live with greater
spontaneity and pleasure.

*Today, I accept what's good, even though
it may not be perfect.*

 *April 23*

If you assume that there's no hope, you guarantee that there will be no hope.

NOAM CHOMSKY

At times our prospects look bleak. Whether what concerns us is a loved one's health, a work problem, or conflict in a relationship, we may be convinced that the future will bring only disappointment. What we've forgotten is that we've already survived many of life's ups and downs. We've lived through some of our worst times and now can use our experience to gain a new perspective.

Surprisingly often, life rewards us with more good than we expected. Even loss and grief are followed in time by the opening of our hearts, gratitude for what we've been privileged to experience, and pleasure in renewed aliveness. All we need concern ourselves with is this day. Though we don't know what tomorrow will bring, we can trust that our Higher Power and the process of life itself have gifts in store for us, if we're open to them.

Today, hope illuminates my day.

April 24

If homosexuality is a disease, let's all call in queer to work. "Hello, can't work today, still queer."

ROBIN TYLER

Some still imagine our lives as perverse, obsessed with sex. In truth, most days we're as occupied as so-called normal people with the work we must do. Many of us work at home, caring for partners, aging parents, and sometimes children; many of us have workplaces where we consistently show up and do a creditable job. We work in vast numbers and varieties of fields, contributing to art, science, government, finance, education, medicine, social work, technology, and more. There are many occupations in which we're still invisible, required to keep our sexual identity "in the closet" if we want to keep working at what we love.

It's been many decades since the American Psychiatric Association agreed to remove homosexuality from its manual of mental disorders. Homophobia has at last begun to leave the workplace and is still in the process of change. It's time for all of us—lesbian, gay, bisexual, and transgender—to stop accepting the ways our sexuality is still stigmatized, give ourselves full permission to be, and proudly embrace our identities.

Today, I appreciate my talents and my valuable contribution to the world of work.

 *April 25*

> *once you'd*
> *get there you'd*
> *remember and love me*
> *of course I'd*
> *be gone by then I'd*
> *be far away*

MAY SWENSON

It's easy to feel inadequately loved by others if we're withholding love from ourselves. Yearning and waiting for understanding to come from outside sources can only bring disappointment. When we place ourselves in a dependent position, we perpetuate our feelings of helplessness and resentment. Having rejected ourselves, we're not surprised when we're rejected by others. And of course we find it hard to give others what we ourselves most crave. We're trapped in a cycle of scarcity and withholding.

It's wonderful to receive validation from others, but we need our own validation most of all. We need to become experts at showering ourselves with unconditional love. The more we love and approve of ourselves, the more we'll find our attitude mirrored by those around us. We'll be able to receive the abundance of love that has been here waiting for us all along.

Today, I offer myself the love I've been waiting for.

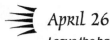 **April 26**

*Leave the battle to God and rest your head
upon your hand.*

YORUBA PROVERB

We have the sense sometimes that life is a series of
conflicts. We speak of the war against AIDS, the
war on drugs, and the war between men and
women or straight and gay people. We describe
our daily chores and problems as battles to be won
or lost. The stakes are high, the forces unequal, the
outcome unpromising. The hostile world outside us
is mirrored by the conflicting forces within us. At
our most stressed, we may feel as if we're warding
off chaos or craziness.

In the words of those in Twelve Step recovery,
we can "show up for life." We can work effectively
without always taking on the stress of living as if
besieged. Rest is not the enemy of action. Serenity
comes when we remember that we're in control of
our decisions and actions, not of their outcomes.
The alternative to doing battle is not to give up and
become passive, but to take appropriate actions and
turn over the results to our Higher Power. Inner
poise and a sense of peace come from knowing the
difference between things we can and can't control.

Today, I rest from my battles.

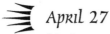 *April 27*

It took me years to figure out that there was anything odd about having the band play "Strangers in the Night" for the bride and groom to dance to at our wedding.

REGGIE
a lesbian in recovery

Some part of us is aware of everything and is ingenious at finding ways to express the truth. From physical reactions to spontaneous wit, we have an array of expressive techniques for revealing such deep truths as sexual orientation or gender identity, whether we're aware of what we're saying or not. For some of us, our sexuality was a secret so well buried that even we ourselves couldn't see it. For others, our dependence on addictive substances or behaviors was unthinkable—so we lacked the ability to think of it.

Sexuality, unacknowledged addiction, abuse or violence in a relationship—many of us have secrets we're holding under pressure at a depth, finding ways to act them out in our lives. Perhaps we're being loyal to a family or personal tradition that requires us to deny some problem that has nagged at our consciousness for years. Secrets don't go away. It's time for us to look at what we've been keeping hidden from ourselves and others.

Today, I'm willing to face my secrets.

 *April 28*

The anarchist painter is not the one who will create anarchist pictures, but the one who will fight with all his individuality against official conventions.

PAUL SIGNAC

We may have looked for ways to fit into the gay, lesbian, bisexual, or transgender community that has become our new context. We look for clues to what appearance, attitude, and behavior will earn approval from our peers or simply the safety of anonymous group membership. Some norms are hotly discussed; others tacitly agreed on. What one group insists upon, another group scornfully opposes. Many detach from such controversies, which have no bearing on their desires or self-image. Our conformities, thankfully, keep changing. We must listen to and respect those who dare to be true originals. In claiming our identities, we needn't adopt new compulsory behaviors in place of those we've discarded. We can explore our most individual and idiosyncratic selves and express them honestly.

Today, I have integrity. I present myself as I am.

April 29

Your disease wants you to blame other people for how you feel.

Man in recovery

Addiction in our lives isn't necessarily obvious. It can start subtly, as something we do for pleasure or recreation; perhaps "everyone" we know does what we do—or so we like to think. We may abstain from addictive substances yet be hooked on caretaking, overresponsibility, and resentment at how underappreciated we are. We may be addicted to a process like overspending, gambling, or workaholism, yet keep "getting away with" the consequences.

Addiction is a way of numbing our sense of responsibility, of forgetting how our choices and decisions got us here, and of ignoring their impact on our health, self-esteem, and emotions. As lesbian, gay, bisexual, and transgender people, we're at higher risk for addiction. We are entitled to break the stereotype and embrace lives of recovery. However we got here, we alone are responsible for making the decision to change.

Today, I take responsibility for my feelings.
I look honestly at my relationship to addiction.

 *April 30*

*and if i ever touched a life,
i hope that life knows that i know that
touching was and still is and always
will be the true revolution.*

NIKKI GIOVANNI

Can we make room for another person in our lives?
Perhaps our idea of compatibility is one in which
another person is our mirror image, rarely challenging our thinking or behavior. Having intimate relationships means accepting that others are separate.
Allowing ourselves and our partners to function in-
dependently and be different gives us both breathing room. It's essential if we are to flourish.

As we gradually allow someone into our lives,
we can use creative visualization to help create a
positive relationship. First, we visualize ourselves
alone at work or play, happy and well, enjoying our
surroundings and ourselves. We use all our senses
to create a full, loving picture. We then visualize the
other person harmoniously interacting with his or
her chosen environment. After vividly imagining
each one separately, we see them greeting each other
and enjoying some shared activity, with room for
each to breathe. We bless and release both people.

*Today, I respect and enjoy another person's autonomy
and my own.*

May 1

While you live you dare not speak; when you die, you cannot.

YIDDISH PROVERB

As lesbian, gay, bisexual, or transgender people, we may not have felt truly seen or listened to in the past. Perhaps we've reacted by always seeking the spotlight, taking center stage whenever we can—or perhaps we've chosen the opposite, retreating into introspection and isolation. We may fear to put our thoughts into words, but we must speak our own truth. Telling the truth aloud is a gift to ourselves and others.

When we take Step Five, we speak to our Higher Power, ourselves, and another human being. We truthfully share what we've discovered in taking a searching personal inventory. The result is a sense of freedom and forgiveness. When we speak and are heard, we know that we belong to the human family. We are similarly blessed when another person trusts us enough to be truthful with us.

Today, I dare to speak the truth. I can be trusted to listen.

May 2

Your feeling of being unforgiven and unforgivable is what makes you suffer so. But it only exists in your heart or mind.

SOGYAL RINPOCHE

Step Five shows us the way to self-acceptance and self-esteem as we acknowledge to our Higher Power, to ourselves, and to a trusted person all those things we wish we'd done differently. The prospect of laying bare our whole past may seem formidable to us at first, but when we risk doing it, we can begin to change.

We can learn to forgive ourselves when we understand that we're not alone in our feelings or actions, that we are forgivable, and that we have already begun to change from the moment we became willing to admit the exact nature of our wrongs. The burden of guilt and shame is lifted from us when we let in the unconditional love of people we trust. Like all human beings, we are entitled to it.

Today, I forgive myself.

May 3

Is it necessary to have read Spinoza in order to make out a laundry list?

JEANNE DETOURBEY

Each day presents us with decisions. Most are relatively small—what to eat or wear or read, how to organize our tasks, with whom to spend time. But at times we face life-changing decisions: where to live or work, whether to undertake more education, whether to commit ourselves to a relationship.

We can view each choice as an opportunity to express our freedom, our unique character, and our ease with ourselves. We needn't fear that we'll make a "wrong" decision. Our mistakes are our teachers; they are essential to our process of growth and understanding. Whether our decisions come from common sense, intuition, the voice of inner guidance, or our Higher Power, our answers are already inside us. We can be confident in our innate ability to make the right choices.

Today, I make both large and small decisions with confidence.

May 4

*When one considers oneself valuable one will take
care of oneself in all ways that are necessary.*

M. SCOTT PECK

As lesbian, gay, bisexual, or transgender people,
we've lived through rejection and hostility, surviving to embrace our unique identities. But there's
more than just survival. To clarify and work toward
personal and community goals, to live the lives we
aspire to, requires that we pay serious attention to
our need for mental and physical nourishment. It
requires cherishing ourselves enough to say no to
habits and circumstances that lower our self-esteem
and sap our energy. It means choosing to thrive, instead of merely getting by. We can take an inventory
of our physical, emotional, and spiritual needs and
ask ourselves what's missing from our current program of self-care and what obstacles keep us from
healthy change. The point is not to revise everything in one day. We can commit to a gentle but
consistent path of improved attention to caring for
ourselves.

*Today, I'm willing to take a step toward caring for
myself more appropriately. I am worth it.*

May 5

Get a small notebook—
write down in it what you want—
JAMES SCHUYLER

We sometimes postpone things we want to do,
waiting for ideal circumstances or more comfortable means. Often, all we need to make a start is the
willingness to begin. Writing is an example; many
of us say, "I'd like to write, but I don't have the
time." We can take a few moments to write today—
right now—without committing ourselves to keeping a journal for the rest of our lives. We don't need
a computer, a writer's studio, or a grant; any pad or
notebook will do.

Instead of living with the frustration of
grandiose schemes, we can cultivate small habits
that move us gradually in the direction of fulfilling
our desires.

Today, I take one small action that furthers
the fulfillment of a desire.

May 6

But this is your time—your time to delve, to dig,
to plow the rich, fertile earth of yourselves.
There you will find every answer worth giving.

MUMIA ABU-JAMAL

When we feel pulled in different directions, whether by demands from outside ourselves or by our own conflicting needs, we need to locate the center of our being. There we will find clarity and energy to face whatever the day requires.

There are many brief exercises that can help focus attention on your center. Some combine attention to breathing with a simple movement. Here is one example: Stand, feet firmly on the floor a short distance apart, spine relaxed but straight, and place both hands on your abdomen or the area just above it—literally, your center. Palms lightly resting on the body, sense the energy within—the life force that in Sanskrit is called *prana* and in Chinese, *chi*. It includes our thoughts as well as our physical bodies. Inhaling deeply, slowly sweep both arms upward, palms and eyes facing the ceiling as you raise your head up and back. Exhale, slowly bringing hands and gaze back to rest on the abdomen. After repeating this movement three to six times, you'll feel more relaxed, poised, and centered.

Today, I stay in touch with my
physical and spiritual center.

May 7

*I think it pisses God off if you walk by the color
purple in a field somewhere and don't notice it.*
ALICE WALKER

A sense of gratitude is something we can cultivate
and choose to express in our lives. Gratitude is an
act of the spirit that lifts us out of our preoccupa-
tion with our problems, large or small. When we
begin to name things we're grateful for, we overcome our sense of difficulty, lack, or resentment.
We can make a gratitude list each day, starting
today. At the beginning or end of the day, we write
a list of five or more things for which we feel grateful—perhaps beginning with this day itself and the
opportunity to live it. Each day, in making our gratitude list, we try to include something, no matter
how small, that we've never listed before.

Awareness of our gifts makes us more generous
toward ourselves and others and more aware of the
action of a Higher Power throughout our day. The
abundance of life flowing around and through us
begins to fill us with joy.

Today, I am grateful.

May 8

*The little ones leaped and shouted and laugh'd
And all the hills echoed.*

WILLIAM BLAKE

On any given day, we're likely to experience problems. Someone may hurt us, something may upset our plans, or we may meet with a hardship or loss. And on any given day, we're also likely to experience happiness. A smile may flood us with a sense of love, we may take time to notice growing things, or we may have the privilege of helping another person.

Remembering that each day contains positive moments, we can anticipate and be present for them and let them lift our spirits. We can keep our attention open to the unexpected, letting small moments of joy fill our consciousness as they come. In this way, we can influence the shape of our emotional life throughout the day. Our emphasis on the positive aspects of our experience uplifts others as well as ourselves. Our expectation of good invites more of what's positive to come to us throughout the day.

*Today, I focus my attention on what is positive
in each of my experiences.*

May 9

*I didn't come out because I fell in love with
another woman. I came out because in therapy
the layers of pain that began forming when I
was eight fell away.*

BLAKE C. AARENS

We may think of progress as something that comes
from striving and hard work, from directing our energies outward. We may believe that our true nature
won't be fulfilled until we find our soul mate. In
truth, we are already complete. We aren't required
to add the right things or people to our lives before
we can be whole.

There's the well-known story about the great Re-
naissance sculptor Michelangelo: when asked how
he created his powerful, lifelike statue of David, he
replied that he had simply cut away from the block
of marble "all that was not David." In our process
of growth and recovery, we find the truth of who
we are under layers of old negative feelings and beliefs about ourselves. As fear, resentment, pain, and
self-rejection fall away, our essence is revealed in all
of its beauty, strength, and confidence.

*Today, I let go of something that is not me,
as part of the process of finding my whole, true self.*

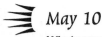 *May 10*

*Whatever we may say we believe, our actions . . .
are the more accurate measure of what we really
believe.*

GUY KETTELHACK

Our lesbian, gay, bisexual, and transgender communities and the recovery programs in which we
participate offer frequent opportunities for us to affirm our loyalty to one idea and proclaim our dislike of another. Whether we're people who avoid
conflict or who like to jump into controversial dis-
cussion, we can bring real change into the world
only by living our beliefs.

We're more likely to help others to come out by
being open about our sexuality than by talking
abstractly about the need for courage. We're more
likely to help others maintain sobriety by practicing
the principles of a Twelve Step program than by
talking theoretically. Taking actions that embody
our beliefs furthers our own growth and development and serves others as a powerful example. The
actions, small and large, that we choose to take are
shaping our characters and our lives.

Today, I translate a belief into an action.

May 11

> *I can bear witness only to the things which I myself
> endured and saw.*

PRIMO LEVI

Each of us has a unique body of experiences,
whether of suffering or of joy. In sharing with others what our past was like, we increase the store of
truth in the world. It's a kind of generosity not to
edit the truth by making things better or worse than
they were. We help make it possible for others to
identify with us emotionally and to remember
events they've forgotten—to clarify the nature of
their own experiences.

Honest sharing is a tool of healing and recovery
for ourselves and for those with whom we trust our
truth. When we bear witness today, whether in
speaking to members of our chosen family, to the
larger community, or to a lover or friend, we are
setting a powerful example that helps liberate us
and the people who hear us.

Today, I bear witness to my own experience.

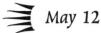

May 12

*Now and then, some of us are ... tempted
just to give up, and go back to the old misery.*

Living Sober

The pull of habit is powerful, and that of addiction
almost irresistible. Our intellectual knowledge of
what's good for us, even our experience of greater
well-being after we've let go of old behaviors for a
time, sometimes can't compete with the powerful
lure of our old dependencies. Fortunately, we have
equally powerful tools and resources to support
new ways of being and acting. "No" is not the only
word in our arsenal; the word "help" can keep us
from isolation.

Attending a recovery meeting, telephoning a
sponsor or trusted friend, praying for assistance
from our Higher Power, reading spiritual or recovery literature, writing in a journal, doing a walking
or chanting meditation, working one of the Steps,
making a gratitude list—any one of these actions
helps us not to have to struggle alone. Admitting
that we're powerless over an old dependency can be
the door that gives us access to the power of our
communities and our spiritual tools.

Today, I can ask for help.

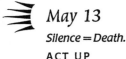

May 13

Silence = Death.

ACT UP

Each of us has our own intuitions and sense of timing about when to come out and to whom. No one should take from us the privilege of naming ourselves in the circumstances and at the times when we're ready. But what about the cost of other silences we've imposed on ourselves? There are many senses in which "silence equals death." If we keep from sharing with family members or friends the fact that we're ill, lonely, or in need, we're depriving them as well as ourselves of connection and choice. If we're holding back from expressing our wants and feelings in a relationship, we're stunting the growth of intimacy. Speaking our truth is an act of humility as well as courage. We can't control the effect on someone else of what we share with them, but we can prevent our own spiritual suicide by refusing to keep silent.

Today, I choose life by speaking my truth.

 *May 14*

Anthropologists have found societies in which people appear to believe in more than two genders. . . . Writer and scientist Martine Rothblatt, who describes herself as a "transperson," has advanced the hypothesis that there are at least as many possible genders as there are shades of color and that people should be free to select a unique gender identity and change it at will.

LEE HUDSON AND STEVE HOGAN

For some, the concept of gender is one more limitation from which we can choose to liberate ourselves. Perhaps we can learn to be more flexible in other ways, too. We may be able to trust our intuition more deeply, feel confidence where we've always been convinced we were incompetent, or become open to someone we've dismissed out of prejudice. Perhaps we can discard an old role that we've been loyal to, allowing ourselves to express more strength or tenderness. The transgender community offers powerful examples of courage, imagination, and expression. We can let go of our restricted assumptions about ourselves and begin to paint an imaginative, new portrait of who we are and would like to become.

Today, I expand my concept of who I am.

May 15

Freedom is indivisible.

JUNE JORDAN

The freedom to be openly lesbian, gay, bisexual, or transgender is closely connected with freedom to know and celebrate ourselves as members of a particular ethnic group or as people of color. We have the right to participate fully in this society without erasing our uniqueness or complexity through assimilation. We have the right to live without the oppression of the closet. Those who identify as bisexual, like those with interracial or multiracial identities, must not be required to efface their many-sidedness. There is more variety and complexity to each of us than any of the labels suggest. Denying part of who we are for fear of not fitting someone else's view is a kind of suicide. Now is the time to live in this new heterogeneous world, all of us participating in the process of liberation, with all parts of ourselves intact.

Today, I have many names, and all of them are mine.

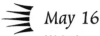 *May 16*

*We're here. We're queer. We're (not) going
shopping.*

QUEER NATION
San Francisco chapter

Sometimes mainstream culture attempts to trivial-
ize who we are and what we've struggled to become
by focusing only on superficial aspects of our lives.
We, too, may be tempted to limit our representation
of lesbian, gay, bisexual, or transgender life by re-
sorting to stereotypes or by undervaluing our depth
and strength.

We're entitled to take ourselves seriously, both as
individuals and as participants in a rich and unique
culture. Our history is filled with achievements far
beyond merely surviving. We have made and kept
worthy commitments. We know the meaning of
love, support, courage, and creativity. We must resist the temptation to think of our needs and accomplishments as inferior. We can remember to accord
ourselves the same respect that we would give to any
other human being. Others will respond to and mirror the respect with which we treat ourselves.

Today, I have dignity.

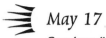

May 17

One doesn't discover new lands without consenting to lose sight of the shore for a very long time.

ANDRÉ GIDE

When we've let go of our old certainties but aren't yet established securely in the new, we may be afraid we'll flounder forever. During periods of indecision or risk—when we've let go of an unfulfilling job or relationship, for example, or when we've admitted powerlessness over an addiction—we don't have to retreat into doubt or fear. Now is the time to let go of our reservations even more completely.

We're not reckless; we've made the decision to enter unmapped territory because of a deep need for change. Our inner wisdom is with us; we can take a deep breath and listen. We can remember that others have made changes like ours and are fulfilled and happy. We can have faith that our Higher Power has not brought us this far only to abandon us. We can feel exhilaration, surrendering the need to control our process of change. We can open to surprise, inspiration, and success beyond our expectations.

Today, I'm patient with the process
as I continue on my chosen path.

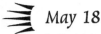 *May 18*

In that case, what is the question?

GERTRUDE STEIN
on her deathbed, after first asking,
"What is the answer?"

Sometimes, we're thrown off balance by another
person's questions—or by the confidence of his or
her assumptions. Our certainties may be shattered
when the way we see our identity, circumstances, or
commitments seems to be called into question. We
don't have to come up with an answer simply because we have been questioned. Instead of rushing
to defend ourselves when we feel put on the spot,
we can take a deep breath and stop to consider
what it is about ideas and beliefs different from our
own that challenges us. We have choices about how
to respond. Some circumstances require that we
simply state our own truth, others that we protect
ourselves from an invasion of our boundaries, and
still others that we keep an open mind and consider
broadening our point of view. We can take time to
decide which response is appropriate.

*Today, I don't react; I respond from my
understanding of the truth.*

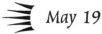 *May 19*

*I suppose I began to drink heavily after I realized
that the things I wanted most in life for myself and
my writing were simply not going to happen.*

RAYMOND CARVER

We may have a picture in our minds of what, for us,
would be failure. When we surrender to the idea of
failure, we're putting things we can't control in
charge of our happiness.

There's nothing wrong with setting goals; goals
contribute to our success by firing the imagination,
giving us a vision of what we're working for. But
when our goals depend on people and events over
which we're powerless, we may be setting ourselves
up for unnecessary and unrealistic feelings of failure. For today, our goal can be simply to show up,
do the best we can, and turn the results over to a
Power greater than ourselves. We can take more
pleasure in the moment-to-moment experiences of a
process when we're not focused on judging the outcome. We can congratulate ourselves for having the
courage to take risks and follow through.

*Today, I honor myself for working toward my
goals to the best of my ability.*

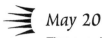 *May 20*

The reward of a thing well done is to have done it.

RALPH WALDO EMERSON

Many of us voluntarily assume extra responsibilities in our workplaces, homes, communities, or families of choice. Perhaps, though we may not be able to acknowledge it, we hope to be repaid in some way. It's useful to take a look at the motives underlying our giving. When we offer service to an organization, a recovery program, or a friend or family member, we may secretly expect that our good deeds will be rewarded by acclaim, popularity, or love.

When we can let go of any hidden agendas for our giving, we're blessed. The more freely and generously we give of ourselves, the freer we are of stress, resentment, and burnout. If we've taken on more than we can handle, if we've lost the appetite for giving, if we're always counting the cost, it's time to look searchingly at our expectations. When we are able to give from our love for others, our hearts expand with joy.

Today, generosity flows from me.

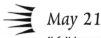 *May 21*

It felt important to me to suggest to people that they not share the core of their vision with anyone but to keep it in their hearts, a sacred gift.

ANNA RICHARDSON

We've become accustomed to freely sharing the details of our experience, strength, and hope with others in recovery programs and in lesbian, gay, bisexual, and transgender communities. We may believe that we have no right to maintain privacy concerning some aspects of our process.

While much healing has come from our own and others' sharing, we are not required to speak our truth to everyone in all circumstances. We don't have to answer every question that is asked. We have the right to be discriminating when we speak of what is sacred to us. We can trust ourselves to know the difference between withholding truth out of fear and choosing silence in order to protect our developing vision and identity. We are entitled to maintain privacy whenever and wherever it feels right for our unique process of growth and healing.

Today, I have the freedom of privacy.

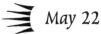

May 22

I am so tired of people whining about what might happen to them, never taking no chances or doing anything new.

DOROTHY ALLISON
Bastard out of Carolina

Standing still and complaining hasn't brought us where we are today. Still, it sometimes feels like part of our process. We all experience times of worry, fear that things won't change, and doubt that we have what it takes to make a difference. When these feelings arise, we don't have to remain stuck in negativity. We can review our journey so far, remembering positive actions we've taken, help we've accepted, and unexpected joys we've been blessed with.

We've taken risks to explore and fulfill our unique natures as lesbian, gay, bisexual, or transgender people in the face of discouragement by society. We've helped one another to heal, celebrate, and create. We've evolved resources, both practical and spiritual, for facing epidemics of sickness and loss. We can continue our journey of faith, willingness, and action, buoyed by our expectation that good will continue to bless our lives.

Today, I turn a worry or complaint around by taking positive action. I have faith in a good outcome.

May 23

Only human beings find their way by a light that illuminates more than the patch of ground they stand on.

PETER AND JEAN MEDAWAR

What is it that fills some of us with faith, while others are full of fear and anxiety? Not only in our communities, but within ourselves, trust in a Higher Power sometimes battles with doubt that our lives have meaning and hope.

Faith is not a substance of which there's only a limited supply, available to some but not others. We can create and nourish faith by taking actions. One of the most powerful is simply to put ourselves in an atmosphere of faith: a Twelve Step meeting, spiritual retreat, healing circle, or religious service. The effects on us of meditation, prayer, or ritual are amplified when we practice them together. Hearing others speak from their faith kindles and supports our own. Alone, we can cultivate the habit of prayer or of reading spiritual literature as if we were exploring a new relationship, suspending judgment, seeing what comes to us from listening and reaching out to Spirit.

Today, whatever my doubts or fears, I act as if I have faith. I stay open to the unfolding of a relationship with my own spirit.

May 24

there's a woman living
deep inside of you
dying
to come out
now don't you be so hard on her
she hasn't been alive as long as you.

SUSAN CAVIN

The old and the new coexist within us. Some days, the voice of the new is strong. We can hear the part of us that wants recovery from addiction or abuse, that has a vision of change in our work and relationships, that wants to be expressed more completely, or that is quietly growing in dignity and self-affirmation. On other days, the new is all but silenced by the loud voice of our old ideas. We can create more hospitable conditions for our new selves by remembering to be gentle with ourselves and patient about our rate of progress. We can seek out people, places, and things that support what is new and positive in our lives. Once new visions have taken root within us, we need not fear that they will disappear. Continuing growth and change are inevitable, as long as we keep listening to the new voice within.

Today, I am willing to let go of an old negative idea and encourage my new self to speak.

 *May 25*

*We were considered magical
by some people. We were considered mysterious.*

JIM EVERHARD

Lesbian, gay, bisexual, and transgender people have
not always been feared or hated in the past. There
has been a range of responses to our orientations
and behavior, including the belief, in some cultures,
that we had magical or shamanic gifts. For example, there are Native American words, such as the
Dakota *wingkta* and the Navajo *na'adleeh,* for
those believed to possess both male and female
spirits. Most Native American groups treated us
with respect, and in some, we were revered as healers. In our own time, there are places where we are
recognized and respected as especially innovative
and sensitive. We are not despised everywhere and
by all people—far from it.

   When we, too, refuse to fear or reject any part of
ourselves or one another, a very real kind of magic
occurs. We help change the balance of acceptance
and understanding in the world. We add to the
world's capacity for love. Our numbers are great
and widespread, and our potential to influence the
world for good is infinite.

*Today, I recognize the power of my own attitude;
I am willing to increase unconditional love and
acceptance in the world by offering it to myself.*

May 26

I can always be distracted by love, but eventually I get horny for my creativity.

GILDA RADNER

We may associate the word *creativity* with a gift for bringing a poem, film, new business, or web site into being. But whether or not we work in a field we think of as creative, each of us has an enormous capacity for creativity and the need to express it in some aspect of our lives.

We all have the gift of imagination and daily opportunities to use it. We can pay attention to details as we create surroundings at home and work that speak to us. We can fill a page beautifully as we write a letter or list. We can appreciate color and texture as we plan a meal or choose what we'll wear. We can seek ways to bring freshness into our relationships, attitudes, and responses. One of the most powerful uses of our creativity is to visualize ourselves and our environments in new ways. In doing this, we collaborate with our Higher Power in increasing the world's supply of peace, hope, and love.

Today, I find an opportunity to use my creative imagination.

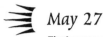 *May 27*

Find someone like yourself. Find others.

ADRIENNE RICH

Whether as lesbian, gay, bisexual, or transgender people or as those recovering from addictions, we are supported by our friendships and associations with others who identify themselves as we do. While we aren't limited to our kinship communities, we're strengthened by coming together with others whose experiences, commitments, and aspirations reflect our own.

Perhaps a dependency or an obsession has made our world narrow, or perhaps we feel the loneliness of an identity that has often been despised. The beginning of the end of isolation comes when we first reach out to another human being, willing to know him or her and to let ourselves be known. We can do so in safety within groups of people who accept and even celebrate who we are. As our chosen communities embrace us, we, too, can extend a welcome to newcomers and others like ourselves.

Today, I am strengthened by being part of a supportive community.

 *May 28*

*I realized I was going to survive this loss.
I learned that no matter how great my pain,
or how alone and frightened I feel, I have
only to remember.*

RAYMOND BERGER

When we're suffering, we may think that we're
never going to feel relief. We may forget that we
have already survived our past, and that joy has
followed pain over and over again. We may neglect
to use the resources within us and surrounding us
that can help through times of pain. Prayer, creative expression, visiting nature, sharing feelings
with people we trust, giving help and service to
others, even performing simple meditative tasks
like washing dishes or sweeping a floor—all these
have helped put broken hearts back together.

To be alive is to feel. We don't have to numb or
deny our feelings of pain or loss. We can respect
and acknowledge whatever we're feeling without
fear. In time, we are healed.

*Today, I remember that I have always lived through
pain. I remember the many resources that help me
to heal.*

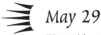 *May 29*

*The eskimos got thirty different names for snow,
I say. I read it in a book.*

*I've got a cousin, Rachel says. She got three
different names.*

SANDRA CISNEROS

There is such diversity within our community that
at times we may be confused by the differences
among us. What does an African American lesbian
poet have in common with a gay white male college
professor? What does the experience of a female-to-
male transgender twenty-year-old have to do with
that of a bisexual woman going through meno-
pause? Instead of quickly categorizing and dismiss-
ing one another, let's take in the richness of our
diversity. Let's respect what others have to share
with us. We can learn from Twelve Step fellowships, where the pain of addiction and the joy of
recovery are not merely personal but are shared in
common, where emotional identification with others is a powerful tool of healing and growth. Let's
go beyond tolerance, beyond merely paying lip
service to the idea of community at once-a-year
Pride events, and reach out to read, listen, and
understand one another's experiences and dreams.
Then, we will truly celebrate ourselves and each
other.

*Today, I reach out to understand and appreciate
lives that are different from my own.*

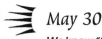 *May 30*

We know "family values" very well. We preserve them.

MALCOLM BOYD

We've discovered, as members of our communities, how much love and loyalty we have to share with other lesbian, gay, bisexual, and transgender friends and with people in recovery. Whatever our needs or problems, there is someone willing to share his or her wisdom and expertise with us; however lonely we feel, there is someone we can call who will try to understand what we're going through. When we have the willingness to reach out for support, we will find it.

We have much to give others in our communities. We have held out a hand to newcomers, listened to those in pain, helped care for the sick, and shared our talents and visions. We've been staunch in our support of one another and of our shared values. We've protested and celebrated together. We've held each other's hands in healing circles. We know that we can continue to count on others and be counted on. As the message on a pin worn at gay and lesbian rights marches says, "Love Makes a Family."

Today, I cherish my chosen family.

May 31

Without guests, the sweetest and healthiest food tastes bitter to the soul.

MICHEL ABEHSERA

We have loving friends, a supportive community, a path of growth and healing, and habits that help us maintain a relationship with our spirit. When we acknowledge how full and developed our lives are, it's easy and natural to share our wealth with others. Our smiles as we enter a room and greet others, the energy of our positive approach to life, our willingness to listen—all these are nurturing and life-giving to those with whom we come into contact, both friends and strangers.

Giving to others doesn't always have to involve long hours or arduous work. Simply showing up, genuinely paying attention to what someone has to say, and offering a word or look of encouragement can help others feel welcome at the feast we ourselves are nourished by. Generosity comes easily when we see how far we've already come and how rich we truly are in the things that matter most.

Today, I share my life's abundance with others.

June 1

Recovery depends on continuing revelation.

DAVID CRAWFORD

Perhaps we sense that something is still standing in the way of our usefulness to our Higher Power, ourselves, and other human beings. We may be aware of a habit that feels addictive or of fears or resentments that are holding us back, preventing us from fully using our gifts.

Step Six suggests that we become entirely ready for change. This means letting go of our illusions about the ways we limit our freedom and happiness—letting go of any denials or excuses. It means trusting that our attitudes and behaviors are capable of transformation. It does not mean attempting to force situations in which our fantasies of control haven't worked before. Being entirely ready means that we're honest about what hasn't succeeded in the past and that we're willing to accept our Higher Power's help. Genuine honesty and openness to change are the essence of the humility we need in order to grow.

Today, I look honestly at what stands in the way of my life's usefulness.

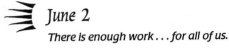

June 2

There is enough work . . . for all of us.

VALERIE MINER

Sometimes we're tempted to think that another's prosperity can only be had at the expense of our own. Good flows into our lives when we let go of the belief that something we desire—material success, recognition, or love—comes in limited quantities. We can then begin to envision plenty for all.

A powerful remedy for feelings of jealousy and lack is to pray for others that they will achieve everything they need and desire. We visualize them as healthy, happy, and fulfilled, praying that life will shower them with all that is good. Our hearts expand with generosity and goodwill. Our sense of being cheated or overlooked leaves us. We remember our unique gifts and opportunities. The blocks to achieving our own success are removed as we fill our minds with images of abundance rather than of limitation.

Today, I have enough.

June 3

You're not given power, you have to take it.

HARVEY MILK

There are times when we wish that friends, family members, romantic partners, and co-workers understood and responded to us with greater awareness and consideration. We expect others to be as sensitive and responsible as we ourselves are: their wants are clear to us, and we try to help. They don't seem to notice that we could use more nurturing or that we have particular wants and needs we would like acknowledged and met.

When we're tempted to harbor feelings of frustration and resentment, we can ask ourselves whether we have indeed stated our own desires clearly or have merely hinted at them, fearing that putting ourselves first might anger or alienate others. When we speak up about what is right for us, others are drawn to our strength. Our clarity results in a greater sense of safety and mutual respect on both sides. We in turn begin to see others more objectively—not as takers or oppressors but as participants with us in an equal dialogue.

Today, it's easy for me to speak about what I need and want.

June 4

*An improviser may have to practice for years
before being able to play a totally spontaneous
minute of music in which every detail is right for
its own fleeting moment.*

STEPHEN NACHMANOVICH

We have achieved mastery and success in some
areas of our lives but are still beginners in others.
We may have forgotten the time and persistence our
accomplishments required and are expecting instant comprehension and command of something
new to us.

It is never too late for us to acquire new learning,
as long as we have the humility and courage to be
beginners again. This means being tolerant of our
own awkwardness and ignorance, being patient as
we go through what seems like failure and not giving up easily on ourselves or on the learning
process. It means persevering, taking small steps
over and over, paying attention to details, and leaving outcomes to our Higher Power. Whether we
want to learn a language, maintain healthy sobriety,
or have satisfying relationships with our peers, the
same combination of openness, consistent action,
and surrender will bring good results.

Today, it's safe for me to be a beginner.

June 5

*Green plants and running water are loved for
themselves, not for the sake of drinking the water
or eating the plants. So too with trees and flowers
and birds: the very sight of them is a joy, and all
joy is loved.*

ABU HAMID AL-GHAZALI

Our love of the natural world can teach us about
our capacity for unconditional love. Earth, water,
plants, and animals inspire us with awe as we appreciate the work of a Power greater than ourselves.
We don't argue with a river because it contains
rocks; we don't think less of a skunk for using its
powerful odor to protect itself. We love the people
in our lives, too, with love that's unconditional.

   Wherever they are in their process of healing and
growth, we can see the beauty and uniqueness of
their spirits. Our love for them doesn't depend on
what they do for us or on how close they are to
achieving their goals. In the same easy way that love
for others, for all that is in the natural world, and
for our Higher Power flows from us, we offer unconditional love to ourselves just as we are today,
with no strings attached. We, too, are part of the
created world.

*Today, my unconditional love for nature, myself,
and others is a source of joy.*

June 6

It takes a certain maturity of mind to accept that nature works as steadily in rust as in rose petals.

ESTHER WARNER

There are times when the world seems uninviting or when we feel as if life has been unfair to us. Life itself, however, is neither fair nor unfair, neither inviting nor dull. Our experience of life depends on our outlook. There are many vantage points from which to view any experience. As lesbian, gay, bisexual, or transgender people, we have some knowledge of how different the world can look when we change our perspective.

If we seek out people, projects, and spiritual practices that we can put our hearts into, the process of our daily lives offers us rich rewards. If we develop a trusting relationship with a Higher Power, we're able to go through times of difficulty, pain, or sadness knowing that what is happening in this moment is not the whole picture. When we accept that some suffering is a part of all of our lives, we feel moved by others' courage in facing their problems and grateful for the healing and growth our own problems make possible.

Today, I accept and embrace the fullness of reality.

June 7

Hard as the recovery process is, it's easier than walking the death spiral of continuing to drink.

BEVERLY WILDUNG HARRISON

Whether or not we define ourselves as dependent on alcohol or any other addictive substance or behavior, most of us know what it is to want to numb our experience and deny a reality that isn't always kind or easy. There are few lesbian, gay, bisexual, or transgender people who haven't sometimes wished for escape from struggle. But avoidance of pain is also avoidance of life. Frequent escapes from reality, repeated attempts to anesthetize our feelings, are like momentary deaths. They can lead to the progression of serious addiction.

When we give in to addictive cravings, each moment is lost to us. Its richness, beauty, challenge, and hope vanish. Even if only temporarily, we become separated from others. Our connection with a Higher Power and with our own spirit is, for the time being, blocked. When instead we embrace the process of recovery, we embrace life in its entirety. We move forward in trust, supported and strengthened by those who have been steadfast in leading sober lives.

Today, I choose life, not death.

June 8

The meeting of two personalities is like the contact of two chemical substances: if there is any reaction, both are transformed.

CARL JUNG

It's been said that no one comes into our lives by accident. We may have a sense that something inevitable and wonderful has occurred when we meet a true friend, mentor, or romantic partner. But just as frequently we encounter people with whom we are incompatible or who seem to threaten our sense of security or self-love. Those people, too, offer us valuable experience. Their presence in our lives requires us to define more clearly our personal values, traditions, and boundaries. They teach us patience and tolerance and help us learn to set limits and speak our truths clearly and assertively. Those who challenge us enhance our process of development. As we express gratitude for the people in our lives today, let's include those who challenge us as well as those for whom our love flows with ease.

Today, I give thanks for all the people in my life, past and present.

June 9

*If I don't paint for one day, I don't feel well
physically or mentally.*

RAPHAEL SOYER

Simple disciplines and routines that we establish in
our lives can be nourishing and health-giving. Taking a morning walk, preparing a healthful break-
fast, writing journal pages, setting aside time for
meditation, attending a meeting of a Twelve Step
fellowship, phoning a sponsor or sponsee—perhaps
our daily routine includes one or more such activi-
ties. At times we may be distracted from the disciplines we've created or tempted to rebel against
them. We may mistakenly equate following a routine with dullness or lack of growth. In fact, the
opposite is true. Routines can serve our recovery,
creativity, and freedom. When our lives are rocked
by change, whether positive or negative, our daily
routines can help us to stay centered. Keeping to
them faithfully sustains and strengthens us.

*Today, I am faithful to routines that support my
physical, mental, and spiritual health.*

June 10

*Why not let reality
simply be
and feel the moment?*

JAIME MANRIQUE

The many responsibilities that keep us so busy are a gift. Living as lesbian, gay, bisexual, or transgender people, we are connected to ourselves and one another through work, love, and dedication to shared ideals. But sometimes obligations seem to overwhelm us. Now is the time for us to step back— not to escape or abandon our commitments, but to gain perspective on ourselves and our lives. Now is the time to reaffirm our relationship with a Power greater than ourselves.

When we take time during the day to enter into prayer or meditation, no matter how briefly, we begin to feel alive, rested, and refreshed. When we stop merely *doing* and quietly contemplate the sights, sounds, smells, tastes, and textures of this moment, it's as if we are taking a deep drink of reality. Our loving relationship with a Higher Power, ourselves, and other human beings is affirmed. We can return to the tasks of our lives with new energy and purpose.

*Today, I take time to step back from activity
and make contact with my spiritual center.*

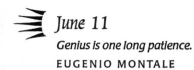

June 11

Genius is one long patience.

EUGENIO MONTALE

Some of us may base our faith on whether or not we're given what we pray for. If a Higher Power hasn't answered our prayers, we wonder what the use is of continuing to have faith. But faith is a matter of surrender, not of control. Let's remember the process we've gone through in order to reach this day. Let's look at some of the many ways life has surprised us so far—not always instantly fulfilling our wishes, but often showing us the path to something more healing and life-giving than what we prayed for.

To live in faith doesn't mean clinging to the self-centered belief that our Higher Power always gives us what we want when we want it. Faith is understanding that there is a purpose and timetable for our lives that we may not yet have the vision and wisdom to understand. Faith is trusting that there are outcomes greater than those we can conceive of. Faith is willingness to leave those outcomes to a Higher Power while—with courage, energy, and patience—we take actions to achieve our goals.

Today, I have faith in my Higher Power's purpose for me.

 **June 12**

Death leaves Us homesick.

EMILY DICKINSON

We have been touched by the deaths of far too many of our peers—people who were on this journey with us and on whom we depended for courage, support, and love. AIDS, breast cancer, addiction, and suicide are among the causes of premature deaths of lesbian, gay, bisexual, and transgender people. We've lost lovers, good friends, family members, and those whose creative visions have enriched and inspired our communities. Our anger and grief are appropriate and necessary if we are to continue living as whole human beings. Our losses are real, but so are our gifts of life and time. Our community continues to grow and our spiritual awareness to deepen. There are those who need us, just as we have needed those we've lost. Our brokenness is part of our strength, as we face and express our rage and pain honestly.

Today, my grief and anger are blessings
as I face my losses.

June 13

This little light of mine, I'm gonna let it shine.

AFRICAN AMERICAN SPIRITUAL

We've been blessed by our leaders and mentors, men and women of originality and vision, people with the courage to come out, speak their truths, and show through the power of their example more about who we are and what we value.

Wherever we have been, whatever we've done, we, too, have our own particular vision and gifts. Our willingness to share our experience, strength, and hope, whether in recovery meetings or our lesbian, gay, bisexual, and transgender communities, is an offering to others like us. We rarely know just what it is that others take away from being with us. As we speak and live our truths, we may be unaware of the importance of the small details that touch, nourish, and begin to heal someone else. Our goal need not be to change others. We must simply let our light shine in the world. Each of us is here for a reason. Each of us is necessary.

Today, I do not hide my light.

June 14

The World is round. Face it.

STANLEY SIEGEL

We have struggled with society's homophobia and with our own internalized shame or fear concerning our lesbian, gay, bisexual, or transgender identity. We may still harbor reservations about our worthiness to be loved. If, in addition, we've struggled with addictive substances or behaviors, we may be more focused on guilt and regret about the past than on our right to affirm our unique gifts.

We can let go of any reservations. Wherever we are in our process of recovery and healing, whatever actions we have yet to take to fulfill our commitment to ourselves, to others, and to a Higher Power, we can recognize that we are following a unique path and have the capacity to live as we were intended: happy, joyous, and free. Willingness is all that we need.

Today, I visualize myself as lovable and whole, a necessary and willing participant in life.

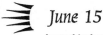 *June 15*

*I need to learn who I am so that I can let go
of behaviors built up around who I am not.*

EAMON FURLONG

Even if we sometimes act as if we lack confidence in
our beliefs, wants, and needs—or in our very identities—there is still a deep part of us that knows who
we are, what we desire, and what we would like
our lives to be. This inner self rebels when we act in
ways that violate our feelings or principles. But the
inner self responds when we recognize our true
selves in our words or actions. If we're still struggling to define ourselves, if we're still repeating old
behaviors that make us uncomfortable, it's time to
listen to the voice of soul. If we wish, we can find
structure and support for our process of growth in
the Twelve Steps, a program that offers a map for
a powerful journey of self-discovery. Over time,
the Steps reveal the original self we've silenced or
denied, restoring us to a sense of wholeness and of
joyous connection with ourselves and others.

Today, in the depths of my soul, I know who I am.

June 16

Successful patients search out possibilities for treatments and cures and follow up every lead they come across. . . . Such behavior leads some doctors to label these patients difficult, noncompliant, or simply obnoxious, but there is reason to believe that difficult patients are more likely to get better while nice ones finish last.

ANDREW WEIL

What is true for many of us dealing with physical illness is also true for those of us seeking to heal our minds and souls. The attitude of faith and persistence and the willingness to assume responsibility for our actions are our priorities. What doubters believe is irrelevant. We want to live full, joyous lives, and we've decided to go to any lengths that recovery requires.

From the moment we decide that we are not hopeless cases, the process of healing has already begun. Negative words cannot discourage us as we take paths we know lead to mental, physical, and spiritual health. We choose the company and support of others who share our belief in what we're doing. We don't hesitate to make fundamental changes in our lives. We love and accept ourselves. We cultivate gratitude for this opportunity for growth and change.

Today, I commit to a path of healing.

 *June 17*

I never hated a man enough to give him his diamonds back.

ZSA ZSA GABOR

Each day of our lives, we're offered gifts. We can learn to see, acknowledge, and treasure them, whatever their source. A glimpse of beauty, a moment of laughter, a creative challenge, contact with a loving friend—all are offerings for which we can be grateful. If instead we walk around with hearts full of ingratitude, resentment, fear, or self-hatred, we are rejecting the life our Higher Power has blessed us with.

It may be easier to recognize sunny days as gifts than rainy ones, but earth and plants need more than one kind of weather to be nourished. If we're going through a period of loss or frustration, of seeming obstacles and disappointments, we can look at what's being offered to us as part of a larger picture. When we contemplate each new experience with the intention of finding something that helps us grow, we will discover it. Instead of living only for the moments when we're given what we hoped for, we can value each day as precious, each experience as a gift we would not wish to return.

Today, instead of rejecting some things and accepting others, I treasure all my experiences as gifts.

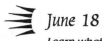 *June 18*

Learn what you are, and be such.

PINDAR

It's difficult for some of us to take a compliment. When others respond favorably to us, we may wonder if they know who we really are; we may believe that if they knew the whole truth, they would think less highly of us.

We are not impostors; we're complex people who are continuing to evolve. We may be competent, sober, generous, and successful and at the same time still have uncertainties and self-centered fears. We can give ourselves permission to be wherever we are in our process of development or recovery. This means acknowledging not only our shortcomings but also our successes. We can value what we've worked to accomplish and become willing to accept others' praise and congratulations without feeling fraudulent. Our progress is real. We can let it empower and nurture us.

Today, my image of myself is positive.
I accept the reality of my progress.

June 19

The sun will set without thy assistance.

THE TALMUD

As lesbian, gay, bisexual, or transgender people—and, for many of us, as people in recovery—we've worked to understand who we are and to bring our lives into alignment with our values. At times we may think we have answers for other people as well. Wanting to be helpful, we may offer unsolicited advice or assume responsibilities that belong to someone else. But we must strike a balance between helping others and letting them help themselves.

When our focus is on others, we may be unconsciously avoiding the next step in our own process of healing and growth as well as preventing others from experiencing the consequences of their choices. One way to honor our lovers, children, friends, and colleagues is to respect the fact that they have their own work to do. We can let others know the impact on us of their behavior, and we can refuse to accept abuse or victimization, but we need not overprotect others by enabling them to avoid responsibility. Like us, they have a purpose in life and a source of inner guidance.

Today, I am not overresponsible.
I keep the focus on myself.

 *June 20*

Make voyages. Attempt them. There's nothing else.

TENNESSEE WILLIAMS

Life may seem like a dangerous proposition to us. We may have had to draw on all our courage, growing up in a homophobic culture; perhaps we've taken the risk of coming out in adult life or have begun the adventure of recovery.

After all we've risked, isn't there some security for us somewhere? Can't we turn to a lover or a job to guarantee us lasting comfort or happiness? There is, in fact, a source of security for us, but it's not located in a person, place, or thing. Safety lies squarely in our relationship with our inner selves and with our Higher Power. When we know we are being true to ourselves and our principles, when we're living according to our convictions, we can be free from the doubts and fears that used to be in charge of our lives. We can trust our vision. We can take responsibility for our actions and let go of the outcome. We can dare to be true originals.

Today, my life is an adventure. In my voyages of discovery, I have the security of knowing my Higher Power is with me.

 *June 21*

Fashions fade—style is eternal.

YVES SAINT LAURENT

It can be difficult to make independent decisions. We may have compared our life choices to those of people around us before taking an action, not wanting to stray too far from whatever our chosen communities deem appropriate at the moment. But whether in matters of appearance, work, sexuality, or politics, we, of all people, do not have to let trends dictate our preferences. We can dare to be one of a kind—authentic, fresh, distinct from those around us.

Declaring ourselves gay, lesbian, bisexual, or transgender in a heterosexist society and opening ourselves to recovery in a culture rife with addiction are actions that take a commitment to our own vision. We can bring this commitment to everything we do. We can trust our intuition about what we ourselves need or don't need in order to be happy.

Today, I am confident. I bring my own flair and originality to the choices I make.

 *June 22*

Deep experience is never peaceful.

HENRY JAMES

Strong feelings, even suffering, are part of the process of finding and liberating our true selves. The awakening of our spirits includes moments of intensity and turmoil, darkness and loss. For us to be willing to undergo such fundamental change as redefining our sexuality or facing a problem of addiction, we may first have had to "hit bottom." But our pain and frustration have had a positive outcome. We've become aware of the impact of our past decisions on ourselves and others. We've let go of denial. We've begun to entrust ourselves to the care of a Higher Power. All that we've gone through has been worth the resulting freedom of self-awareness and self-acceptance. We know ourselves to our very depths. We are entirely at home with ourselves, no matter what we feel.

Today, I am not afraid of intense feelings and experiences as I get to know myself better and better.

June 23

Enjoyment is not a goal, it is a feeling that accompanies important ongoing activity.

PAUL GOODMAN

Joy is a worthy motive for the things we choose to do. In fact, we are meant for joy; we require it. Our Higher Power wants us to have it.

In our pursuit of happiness, we've sometimes mistaken instant gratification for the lasting sense of fulfillment we truly desire. Choosing the "quick fix" of an addictive substance or behavior, sex without meaning, or work motivated solely by the desire for money has left us feeling empty and unsatisfied in the end. When we commit ourselves to a principle, share our gifts with others, invest ourselves in work that feeds the soul, and let our hearts lead us, the happiness we feel is authentic and enduring.

We know, deeply and intuitively, which choices will feed us only for a moment and which will bring lasting joy. Though all our wishes and desires may not be gratified, we can feel the joy that comes from knowing and listening to our souls.

Today, I choose joy.

June 24

Everyone has a talent. What is rare is the courage to follow the talent to the dark places where it leads.

ERICA JONG

Sometimes, when we're in the midst of working out a problem, creating something new, or attempting to make a major change in our behavior, we feel as if we've "hit a wall." The enthusiasm we felt at the beginning of the project, relationship, or recovery program seems to have evaporated. We wonder if we have the energy and inspiration to continue.

This is exactly the moment when we must hold on and persist in our efforts. Our fears of failure are like voices talking to us from the past. We can turn around and face them. We're different people now. We have a network of support we can draw upon. We have enough faith to persist, one day at a time, in what matters to us, even though we're not sure of the outcome.

Our confidence and self-esteem are bolstered by our persistence. Our abilities grow as we refuse to let today's problems discourage us.

Today, I don't surrender to the voice of discouragement. I am persistent.

June 25

What is bestowed by heaven is called human nature. The fulfillment of human nature is called the Tao. The cultivation of the Tao is called true learning.

TZU-SSU

We've come too far in our process of change and self-awareness to deny our true identities and gifts. If we are lesbian, gay, bisexual, or transgender, we know that we must acknowledge and embrace our sexuality if we are to live full and truthful lives. If we have faced the destructive power in our lives of an addictive substance or behavior, we know that we can't go back to denial. If we have discovered the talents that bring us joy, we can't accept a life that doesn't include using and developing them. To reject the inner knowledge of our true nature is to deny body and spirit the nourishment they need and to deny our Higher Power the opportunity for love and expression through us. We sense the purpose for which we were created. It is time to listen to what we already know. It is time to invite our souls to appear at the feast.

Today, I know myself, I accept myself, and I celebrate myself.

June 26

*It is what we all do with our hearts that affects
others most deeply. It is not the movements of our
body or the words within our mind that transmit
love. We love from heart to heart.*

GERALD JAMPOLSKY

Relationships are living things. In addition to romantic partnerships, we have many kinds of relationships, including those with friends, family members, co-workers, sponsors, and sponsees. Each has its reason for being. Each has its own path and process of development.

When we take an inventory of our varied relationships, we're likely to find that the successes and problems we're experiencing are indicative of successes and problems in other areas of our lives. We may feel affirmed in particular relationships. We may cling to relationships in which we're abused as part of a pattern of being victimized in our lives. We may take relationships for granted, neglecting to nurture them with time and expressions of caring; perhaps we have difficulty sustaining other connections, as well. We may feel undeserving of happiness, staying in relationships we know cannot grow. The heart knows whether it is uplifted or cast down, challenged or supported. We know when love flows with ease. We know when we have work to do, in relationships as in the rest of life.

*Today, I look with an open mind at my
role in relationships.*

 *June 27*

Many of the great mothers have not been biological.

ADRIENNE RICH

Some of us had biological mothers who offered unconditional love that strengthened us and fostered our self-esteem, but no matter what our original families were blessed with or lacked, we can find maternal qualities in many places, including some seemingly unlikely ones.

We are here on this earth to love and nourish ourselves and one another and to help manifest our creative visions and social ideals. In our communities are people who understand and support us in this process. Sponsors and peers in Twelve Step programs can help us to learn—or relearn—fundamental ways to care for body and spirit with wholesome food, rest, and fellowship. Those who have been through struggles like our own can remind us to be gentle with ourselves and not to rush our journeys. Members of our lesbian, gay, bisexual, and transgender communities can offer recognition and caring that help us take our visions and talents seriously. And we, too, can offer mother love to others, continuing the circle of nurturing.

Today, I am sustained by others, as I sustain them.

June 28

*And the wild regrets, and the bloody sweats,
    None knew so well as I.*

OSCAR WILDE

Life-changing events such as coming out, entering recovery, facing another's death, or confronting our own mortality can bring us back to a time in our lives that we don't want to remember. When memories surface, we may at first want to escape the pain of reliving things we wish had happened differently. But our mature awareness can help us to refocus and see our past from a new perspective.

When we review our lives with an attitude of compassion, there is nothing we need to fear looking at again. Reminded of the consequences of our previous choices, we can renew our resolve not to repeat behavior that has brought pain to ourselves and others. Sharing our past honestly will serve as a powerful example to others who are suffering.

Good memories, too, have the power to heal. We cherish memories of accomplishment and courage, of loved ones and friends who have nurtured us, and of deep connections that have blessed us.

Today, I have no fear of my memories.

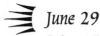 *June 29*

Before enlightenment, carry the water, till the soil.
After enlightenment, carry the water, till the soil.

ZEN PROVERB

We've experienced awakenings of body, mind, and spirit. Having come out as lesbian, gay, bisexual, and transgender people, we see ourselves and the world with new eyes. Those of us in recovery have come to understand ourselves and our primary purpose with greater clarity through taking the path of the Twelve Steps. But enlightenment of whatever kind is nothing in itself if we do not use it to transform our lives. It requires us to live each day as if our insights really mattered. It's in the small, concrete details of our everyday lives that an awakening manifests itself. It's in being present and aware, moment to moment—not dulling our spirits with addiction, not forgetting to share our experience and offer service to others, not neglecting the unglamorous tasks that are necessary to keep our lives in healthy order. Whether our outer routine changes a lot or very little, inside we're alive with the excitement of a soul that loves the world.

Today, fulfilling my ordinary responsibilities is a blessing.

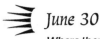 *June 30*

Where there is sorrow there is holy ground.

OSCAR WILDE

The epidemics that affect so many in our community have helped us to understand the reality of death, to create compassionate care for the sick and dying, and to respect our need for grief. Many of us have begun to understand that we are mortal, that there isn't infinite time for our work and relationships.

All of us can begin to have a deeper appreciation of each day and of people we love. We must not live as if it made no difference what we did or with whom. We no longer have time to waste.

The losses in our community are immense, and our mourning is the expression of profound sorrow. But in facing the inevitability of our own and others' deaths, we can free our spirits. As if we've been given a second chance at life, we can approach each day with greater zest and a deeper sense of meaning.

Today, I treat time and people as precious.

July 1

*The difference between a demand and
a simple request is plain to anyone.*

Twelve Steps and Twelve Traditions

Step Seven suggests that we humbly ask a Power
greater than ourselves to remove our shortcomings. To some, the very idea of humility seems
old-fashioned, in conflict with our struggle to
achieve inner strength and confidence as lesbian,
gay, bisexual, and transgender people. But true
humility doesn't conflict with self-trust and self-love.

Humility means recognizing that we ourselves
aren't in charge of how or when our desires for
change will be fulfilled. It means trusting that we're
changing in ways that aren't yet obvious to us. It
means reminding ourselves each day to be patient
and to persevere as we make choices and take actions. It means accepting that we may need time to
adjust to change. Recovery, progress, and maturity
are gradual processes, not one-time events. When
we look back at major transformations we've already experienced, we know we can rely on our
Higher Power to guide us through continuing
change over time.

*Today, I ask my Higher Power to assist me
in my process of healing, growth, and change.*

July 2

Praised be You, my Lord, through our Sister
*   Mother Earth,*
who sustains and governs us,
and who produces varied fruits with
*   colored flowers and herbs.*

FRANCIS OF ASSISI

Many lesbian, gay, bisexual, and transgender
people live in urban environments. We come
together in cities for many reasons, including
opportunities to find one another, to be less
noticeably different in a place where there are
such numbers and such variety, and to find work
in artistic fields. But there are many of us who love
living close to nature—some as carpenters, farm-
ers, horticulturists, craftspeople, innkeepers, or
writers.

    Wherever we choose to live, we can remember
that we, too, are a part of the natural world that sustains us. We can make time in our busy lives to touch
the earth, smell the rain, tune in to the rhythms
of nature that rest and revitalize us, expressing our
gratitude for its beauty and abundance. We can each
take actions, however small, that contribute to the
creation of a cleaner, healthier planet.

Today, I am conscious of being part
of the natural world.

July 3

I seem to have an awful lot of people inside me.

EDITH EVANS

We all know the experience of indecision. When we're torn between two alternatives, we may sometimes feel as if we don't have the right to have such conflict within ourselves. We may force ourselves to make a decision before we're ready.

One way to deal with a dilemma is to embrace it. Rather than pressure ourselves to come to a premature conclusion, we can acknowledge our conflict. We can say simply, "This is a dilemma for me right now. I can't make a decision until I'm clear about what's right for me." Whether a dilemma concerns work or relationships, conflicting pleasures or responsibilities, we need not create the drama of an instant positive or negative reaction. Once we are able to acknowledge our dilemma, it begins to become clear which action is most appropriate for us to take.

*Today, I can allow myself ambivalent feelings.
I can take my time with a decision.*

July 4

*The liberation of homosexuals can only be
the work of homosexuals themselves.*

KURT HILLER

Whether as individuals or as a community, we have
well-wishers and friends from whom we draw support and inspiration. However, for each of us there
are turns in the road where we must strike out in-
dependently. A friend may be uncomfortable with
our choices, lack understanding of our vision, or
even resent our growth; he or she may fear being
left behind.

It's not always possible to please others, and it's
not our responsibility to do so. More difficult, yet
more honest and satisfying, is to understand what
truly pleases *us* and our Higher Power, and then to
make genuine efforts to move in that direction. If
our friends cannot accept and support us, we can
let go without regret. We can breathe deeply of the
fresh air of our independence. We can be certain
that there are others who are moving in new directions as well and who will be happy for us.

Today, I am independent.

July 5

Telling the truth is what brought me in touch with my Higher Power.

Gay man in recovery

We want to speak the truth of our experience, observations, feelings, and desires. But we may fear that if we tell the truth, we'll risk losing something. We may lack sufficient self-esteem to be entirely ourselves with others.

A life of people-pleasing requires that we lie to others and to ourselves. Lying usually backfires in time: our expressions, bodies, and actions eventually reveal the truths we were afraid to face. Instead of separating from others, from our Higher Power, and from our true selves by lying, we can have the courage and self-esteem to tell the truth. The habit of truth-telling in both small and large things nurtures our self-esteem and self-trust. When we live in truth, we can face ourselves and others without fear.

Today, truth brings me closer to myself and others.

July 6

When you feel pain fall into your brothers' love.

LARRY MITCHELL

Some pain, whether physical or mental, is an inescapable part of human life. When we use our talent and energy trying to ward off inevitable pain, we prolong it and add the exhaustion of fear, worry, denial, or resistance to the event or feeling we were hoping to avoid. Some of us have created a life out of avoiding pain, numbing ourselves with addictive substances or behaviors.

By facing pain directly we can limit its power over us and end it sooner. But we don't have to face pain alone. A "stiff upper lip" is not required. We can accept support from our friends, community, or fellow members of a Twelve Step group. When we turn to others we trust and share our pain with them, we find that they, too, have experienced pain, survived, and grown as a result. Knowing this gives us courage.

This, too, shall pass.

Today, I face pain directly. I don't prolong it by trying to avoid it.

July 7

> *If you want to make a difference, if you want to feel good about yourself, find a cause and lend your time and talents. Nothing is more rewarding.*

ELIZABETH TAYLOR

If we are feeling shortchanged by life—feeling that our gifts are insufficiently recognized and rewarded, that our luck and opportunities are somehow never good enough—the best way to free ourselves from self-centered dissatisfaction is to help others. Service doesn't have to be draining or complicated. Doing a mailing for a community organization, reading to the sick, teaching a skill at a gay and lesbian center, and reaching out to newcomers in a Twelve Step program are simple forms of service that transform lives. Service not only helps other people and organizations, it fills us with a sense of purpose and caring. It heightens our self-esteem. It changes our mental and emotional lives, shifting our focus from disappointment to gratitude and a sense of our own abundance. It starts a chain reaction that keeps the energy of love and service flowing.

Today, I make a difference by offering service.

July 8

I have saved no objects to conjure up memories of lost loves and adolescent crushes, and my history must survive in my mind.

ZANNIE KYD

Our gift for remembering can serve us for good or for ill; the choice is ours. As individuals, we cherish memories of loving connection, shared laughter, satisfying work, and uplifted spirits. As a community, we embrace our remembered history of survival and pride. Such positive memories become a part of the way we define ourselves. They can strengthen and sustain us in challenging moments. They can help keep our faith alive.

Even difficult memories can be useful. When we remember actions we took in the past that had a negative impact, we're reminded that we no longer have to repeat the same mistakes. Such memories can be a blessing and a source of freedom.

We have a choice about how we wish to use our minds and where to focus our attention. We no longer need fear our memories of the past, any more than we need fear the future.

Today, I embrace my memories.

July 9

*Our inherently imperfect understanding
helps shape the reality in which we live.*

GEORGE SOROS

Our experience is not something outside of us, not
something that is *done to* us. We can influence the
shape of our own experiences by choosing beliefs
and attitudes. The attitudes of wonder, gratitude,
curiosity, lightness, friendliness, humor, trust, and
a sense of beauty can profoundly affect our perception of a process or an event.

One way to cultivate a positive attitude is to
create our own affirmation about whatever we're
facing and write it several times. Whatever our
negative belief, we can write a sentence that states
its opposite. We use the present tense, as if we already held the new, positive belief we're affirming.
For example, we might change the statement "I'm
afraid of _____" to "I have confidence and courage
as I face _____." Taking a few minutes to fill a page
with our affirmation can help create a new attitude
toward whatever lies ahead of us.

*Today, I change my experience by creating
a positive affirmation.*

July 10

Every atom belonging to you as well belongs to me.
WALT WHITMAN

In focusing on our differences as lesbian, gay, bisexual, or transgender people—dwelling on what
distinguishes us from members of "straight" society
and even from one another—we may lose sight of
all that we hold in common. While it's necessary
and valuable to deepen our connection to our particular identities, causes, friends, and communities,
we do not have to reject others who are outside of
those circles.

As human beings, we share many similar problems and concerns, losses and joys. Our experience
as outsiders can add depth to our understanding of
others' lives. We can offer the healing influence of
our insight and compassion. We can reject our fear
of those we see as different from ourselves and help
lead the way to creating peace and understanding.
We can assert our differences, yet refuse to foster a
sense of separation or enmity.

*Today, I meditate on what I share
with the rest of humanity.*

July 11

En mis sueños	In my dreams
las velitas	the tapers
de mi alma	of my soul
prenden con	light with
esperanzas	hopes

ANA KOWALKOWSKA

When we hope, we are not being unrealistic. We know that miracles are possible and are happening every day. Hope can be a creative force in our lives, leading the way to positive change.

We have seen miracles of change in our own lives. Our desire to live and to connect with others has often been more powerful than sickness, doubt, or despair. Our desire for peace has proved capable of ending inner and outer warfare. We have changed our lives in ways we couldn't have predicted, surviving and thriving in new roles, some of us recovering from addictions, others embracing the truth of our identities and desires. When we work toward positive outcomes even in seemingly unpromising circumstances, we are trusting and cooperating with our Higher Power to create movement and progress.

Today, I cultivate hope in myself and others.

July 12

To enjoy freedom we have to control ourselves.

VIRGINIA WOOLF

We've thrown off many oppressions in the process of embracing our particular identities and, for some of us, in emerging from the prison of active addiction. We want to be happy, joyous, and free. As we seek to fulfill our desires, we may sometimes be confused about the nature of freedom. We may neglect a responsibility or rebel against a commitment that feels as if it's weighing us down. We may be shortsighted, forgetting that our long-term goals require consistent effort. Freedom does not mean being lax, selfish, or resistant. Self-discipline is not the enemy of pleasure. On the contrary, when we are faithful and steady, pursuing our goals with discipline, we enjoy a sense of mastery and self-esteem. We enjoy true freedom.

Today, in the spirit of freedom, I take one step toward keeping a promise to myself through disciplined action.

July 13

*There are four thousand reasons
why I shouldn't pursue this,
starting with
I don't think she likes me.*

ALI LIEBEGOTT

There are times when we do ourselves and others a favor simply by *not* taking an action—*not* making a particular phone call, *not* trying one more time to explain our side of an argument, *not* trying to rescue someone who has ignored offers of help. But, we may ask ourselves, shouldn't we be persistent? How will we ever succeed at anything if we give up so easily?

There are times when leaving things alone is more appropriate—even necessary, if we want to avoid creating pain or resistance. We usually know whether action or inaction is the right answer; it's deep inside us. But when intuition is warning us against action, we have to be willing to listen to it. In Al-Anon, there is a saying: "Do the person you love a favor today: leave him or her alone."

*Today, I know when to leave people and
situations alone.*

July 14

In less than one year, 98 percent of all the atoms in your body are replaced completely. This includes even the DNA, which holds memories of millions of years of evolutionary time. . . . You are literally changing your body as effortlessly as you change your clothes.

DEEPAK CHOPRA

Perhaps we have given up on changing certain aspects of our lives. We may say to ourselves, "This is something I can't change." But when we look back at our old ideas and behaviors, we can see how we have changed. We can see how often change has occurred even without our conscious effort. Change is constant and inevitable in our lives at every level— physical, mental, and spiritual.

Willpower doesn't bring about change, *willingness* does. With willingness and trust in a Higher Power, we can replace old habits with new ones, just as our bodies replace their atoms.

Today, I am willing to change my life for the better.

July 15

Never once, in all those acres of newsprint, had I been asked about my faiths and beliefs, both of which had played important roles in my life. What I slept in, apparently, was considered more important than what I believed in.

CHRISTINE JORGENSEN

Though a homophobic culture may insist on viewing transgender, bisexual, gay, or lesbian sexuality as something humorous, titillating, sick, or disgraceful, we ourselves know that we are whole human beings. We know that there is much more to us than our sexuality and that our sexuality is God-given and beautiful. A profoundly spiritual energy flows through our lives and communities. For those who dare to change what they find unacceptable—even a "given" such as gender identity—courage is not merely the bravado of rebellion, but comes from a deep source of knowledge and spirit within. It is important that we refuse to internalize the view that we, our gender identity, and our sexuality have less dignity or worth than anyone else's. Maintaining daily contact with Spirit strengthens our ability to resist the limited view that we are merely sexual beings.

Today, I am more than my sexuality.
Spirit is my source and my center.

July 16

*You will not find poetry anywhere unless
you bring some of it with you.*

JOSEPH JOUBERT

We can cultivate a sense of the poetry within us.
Smiles and tears, sun and rain, work and rest—
whatever we see, smell, hear, taste, touch, or feel
has its own particular beauty. As we walk through
the day, we can stop and really look at the people
we encounter. We can intuit the desires behind their
words and gestures. We can let our hearts flow out
to others in sympathy. We can hear the day's various sounds, both noisy and subtle, and we can hear
the day's silences. We can let each perception, each
small event, become like a note of music, a word in
a poem, or a dancer's gesture. We can step back and
marvel at the varied, interwoven moments as we
would at a tapestry. When we look, listen, taste,
and touch as creative artists, the day will divulge its
beauty to us.

*Today, I find poetry in the day. My sensitivity to beauty
deepens my experience of everything that happens.*

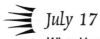 *July 17*

*When I begin to lose track of the path to God,
I must remember to start looking where I know
he lives if he is anywhere: in the sound of laughter.*

MICHAEL LASSELL

Laughter cleanses us of discouragement, anger, apathy, and grief, making room for new feelings and thoughts. Laughter frees us from self-consciousness, anxiety, and stress. Laughter helps heal our physical ailments—it massages internal organs and strengthens the life force flowing through us. Laughter teaches us to take our troubles lightly, releasing our spirits from the weight of the world and of ourselves. Laughter unites what has been separate, connecting us to one another and to our true selves. Laughter calls forth our desire to live. Laughter, then, is a source of miracles. Surely, it's one of the places where we can meet our Higher Power.

Today, I let laughter heal me.

July 18

Quietly sitting, body still, speech silent, mind at peace, let thoughts and emotions, whatever rises, come and go, without clinging to anything.

SOGYAL RINPOCHE

Perhaps in our busy lives we haven't yet been able to find time for the consistent practice of meditation, or perhaps we've tried meditation and haven't experienced its benefits as quickly as we would like. If this is the case, we may wish to reconsider the practice of meditation. Rather than thinking of it as a means to an end and rather than judging our experience of it, we can try to find in ourselves the willingness simply to *be*. Whether for a few minutes or for a long session, we can meditate as easily and thoughtlessly as we breathe, simply allowing life to flow through us as we inhale and exhale without worry or struggle. We can come to meditation as we would come home after a day of work or after a long journey away from what is familiar. We needn't strive for special, heightened experiences; we can enter the calm and serenity of accepting ourselves, our minds, and our surroundings just as they are.

Today, I experience the peace of meditation.

 *July 19*

I am not wrong: Wrong is not my name
My name is my own my own my own
JUNE JORDAN

There is a long list of insults that have been used
for generations to describe people like us. Whether
we've experienced having such names hurled at us
individually or not, we've heard and absorbed
them. We've understood the bigotry and ignorance
they imply. They've taught us the power of words
to influence and shape our experience.

We have a responsibility toward ourselves and
others to name ourselves with conscious care, understanding that names have creative power. Some of us
are inventing new names for the ways we experience
gender or sexuality. Others have reclaimed old, in-
sulting names and adopted them with pride, changing their energy and impact by controlling them.

We can list the many words we use in referring
to ourselves and notice whether the portrait that
emerges is loving or rejecting. We can list alternative words with which to name ourselves as part
of our creation of a positive identity.

*Today, I am conscious of the power of words
to influence reality. I use positive language to
name myself and others.*

July 20

You can do foolish things,
but do them with enthusiasm.

COLETTE

What are the ways in which we're holding back
from wholehearted participation in things that
matter to us? We must evaluate circumstances
and consult our own feelings and needs before
plunging headlong into any situation, but when
we keep postponing things we care about, inaction itself becomes our choice.

Procrastination often is caused by fear. We may
be afraid of making fools of ourselves, believing
deep down that we're "not good enough." We
needn't remain loyal to our old fears. We can stop
denying ourselves full participation in our chosen
paths. When we dare to make a beginning, we're
no longer alone. Our Higher Power is part of the
process. Whether taking small actions or large,
whether in personal relationships or programs of
recovery, at work or play, we can proceed wholeheartedly. Whatever we do with enthusiasm, energy,
and commitment will inspire and transform us.

Today, I don't give my energy to hesitation.
I move forward boldly, with faith in my Higher Power.

July 21

*There is more to be learned from wearing
a dress for a day, than there is from wearing
a suit for a lifetime.*

LARRY MITCHELL

If the culture we've been raised in is sexist in many
of its attitudes, it stands to reason that most of us
share those attitudes to some extent, consciously
or unconsciously. Whether we are lesbian, gay, bisexual, or transgender, chances are we've absorbed
some of the culture's belief that women are inferior.
We may, for example, make or enjoy jokes that disparage women's bodies or aging process; whether
we're men or women, such denigrating humor is an
act of self-hate and self-rejection. We may be intol-
erant of women's continuing struggle for liberation,
caricaturing feminist perspectives as too angry, too
strident, or even "hysterical." When we reject the
legitimacy of any group's claim to liberation and
dignity, we reject ourselves.

Let's look at the rejection within us of what we
call "female" and what we call "male." Let's acknowledge the qualities within us that have traditionally been assigned to one gender or the other.
Let's bring our intolerance of women and of men
into the open and let it go.

Today, I let go of any prejudice against men or women.

July 22

He who would do good to another must do it in minute particulars.

WILLIAM BLAKE

A day that includes acts of kindness adds to our happiness and self-esteem and expands the capacity of our own and others' hearts. It teaches us the art of paying attention. It takes the focus off ourselves. For kindness to accomplish so much, it must be sincere—more than rote politeness. It both requires and creates caring.

Kindness needn't be grandiose. Kindness can be a word or look expressing our appreciation of any-one who is doing a job well: the small courtesy of genuine thanks to the person who bags groceries at the store or to the office maintenance worker clean-ing the lavatory. Kindness can be a friendly greeting on the street, an offer of a seat on the bus, or filling a coffee cup or passing a tissue at a Twelve Step meeting. Kindness to those close to us, too, can be expressed in small acts of gentleness or affection. Kindness does not have to take anything from us. The moment required for a small act of thoughtful-ness is amply repaid by the feelings it creates in us and others.

Today, I notice others;
I perform at least one small act of kindness.

 *July 23*

I have no home except what I make for myself.

MINNIE BRUCE PRATT

As lesbian, gay, bisexual, and transgender people, we may have had to be especially imaginative in finding places where we truly feel at home. We can have a sense of home in many places other than where we sleep and eat. Home is where we feel comfortable with ourselves and others, where we renew ourselves through creativity, communication with loved ones, or simple solitude. It may be a Pride march, a community event, or a Twelve Step meeting where shared ideals and experiences foster a sense of connection with others. Home may be a celebration where we laugh with others or a memorial service where we acknowledge ways a friend has touched our lives. It may be prayer or meditation, where we relax in the peace of our true selves and greet our Higher Power. The place we call home is a place where our spirits can take root, where we can dream in safety. When we are truly accepting of ourselves, we can experience the sense of being at home anywhere.

Today, I am at home wherever I am.

July 24

I do not think that obsession is funny or that not being able to stop one's intensity is funny.

JIM DINE

Our culture romanticizes obsession as something that drives artists, thinkers, and lovers. But when we look at obsession up close or experience it in our own lives, it's entirely different from artistic inspiration, intellectual passion, or genuine love: these all require being responsive to the power of reality.

Obsession gives power to *unreality*. Like addiction, it leaves us no room for choice. It takes charge of our minds and fills us with unwanted feelings. It numbs our spirits and separates us from our Higher Power. Also, like addiction, obsession can only be healed when we become aware of its existence and admit that we haven't been able to control it. Treating an obsession as we would an addictive substance or behavior, we trust our Higher Power to restore us to sanity. We let go of illusions of power. We stop trying to control reality and begin living in it. We experience a wider range of feelings. We begin to connect with other members of the human family.

Today, I know the difference between a passion and an obsession.

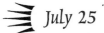 *July 25*

> *It is better to renounce revealed truths, even if
> they exalt us by their splendor or if we find them
> convenient. . . . It is better to content oneself with
> other more modest and less exciting truths, those
> one acquires painfully, little by little and without
> shortcuts, with study, discussion, and reasoning,
> those that can be verified and demonstrated.*

PRIMO LEVI

Listening to a forceful personality trying to per-
suade us of who we are and what we ought to do
can feel like falling under a magic spell. Glamour,
charisma, the power of another's self-assurance—
we may be especially vulnerable to their influence
if we're not yet entirely sure of our own identity
and purpose.

There is nothing wrong with paying attention
to our own lessons of experience. How do we feel
while we are experiencing something? How do we
feel about ourselves after a particular action? What
are its consequences for us and for others? Such
questions can help us sort out what is true for us.
We needn't come under anyone's spell as we remain
faithful to our values and to the voice of our inner
selves.

*Today, I trust the truths I've learned from
my own experience.*

 *July 26*

Money costs too much.

ROSS MACDONALD

It may be tempting to base our feelings of satisfaction on what we are paid or to let money lead us in making important choices. In fact, money can't satisfy our deepest cravings, and the absence of it is rarely our true complaint when we're dissatisfied with a work or personal situation.

Self-esteem requires that we place value on what we do and that we become willing to ask for adequate compensation. Even more important is choosing work that we love, deriving self-esteem from exercising our gifts and serving others. When we must compromise our values and standards for the sake of money, we learn that money indeed costs too much. When we say no to what is wrong for us and yes to our hearts' desires, our Higher Power cooperates with our efforts to work out the financial details.

Today, I do not let money lead me.
I embrace the work I love, trusting that I will thrive.

July 27

In dealing with those who are undergoing great suffering, if you feel "burnout" setting in, if you feel demoralized and exhausted, it is best, for the sake of everyone, to withdraw and restore yourself. The point is to have a long-term perspective.

THE DALAI LAMA

When we care for loved ones who are sick, when we work in helping professions that require us to be constantly available to others, or when we dedicate ourselves to a cause that requires seemingly endless sacrifices, we may experience deep fatigue and a feeling of hopelessness. Instead of struggling to the point of exhaustion, we may need to remove ourselves entirely for a time in order to rest and refresh body and mind. At such times, we needn't draw conclusions or make decisions about the long run. Fatigue is a mood changer and is not a reliable judge of reality. When we have renewed ourselves and revived our morale, we will once again be able to confront suffering with our inner core of generosity and courage intact.

Today, I take time out to refresh my body and spirit.

July 28

There are so many things we could be speaking out about, but it [an injustice] does not seem to have much to do with our daily lives, so we just ignore it.

DANIEL GOLEMAN

When we're uncertain whether or not to speak out about an injustice—unfairness, violence, or abuse— we should consider the sources of our fear. Sometimes, our speaking out poses risks for others. In such circumstances, we refrain from speaking. More often, our silence comes from fear of consequences to ourselves: reprisal, unwanted attention, or embarrassment. Or we lack compassion, forgetting that we are all one family. When we see neglect or pain in our lesbian, gay, bisexual, and transgender family or community, when we recognize injustice in the larger society, we are responsible for naming what we see. Our words and actions, however small, begin ripples of change. When we let go of the idea that we're too insignificant to have any effect or that others' sufferings have nothing to do with our own, not only do we have an impact on those around us, we also strengthen our sense of self and expand our hearts.

Today, unless my speaking might harm others, I break my silence about a wrong.

July 29

*The art of art, the glory of expression and
the sunshine of the light of letters is simplicity:
nothing is better than simplicity.*

WALT WHITMAN

Writers, artists, and gifted teachers communicate
most effectively and memorably when they pare
down a thought or an emotion to its essence. There
is power and beauty in simplicity. Think about the
difference between two store windows: at a five-
and-dime, the window is jammed with too many
things for our eyes to take in at once; at Tiffany's,
a spotlight falls on a single precious object, making
its value obvious at a glance.

In our lives, we, too, can be artists of simplicity.
We can make each day beautiful by keeping it simple. Haste, confusion, and worry never serve us or
others. The chaos of such emotions is like the clut-
ter of extra words or images. As with too many
objects in a store window, they only distract. If we
have several tasks, we can prioritize them in order
of importance. Let's focus on what is most important on this day.

Today, whatever I am facing, I keep it simple.

July 30

Morality is simply the attitude we adopt toward people whom we personally dislike.

OSCAR WILDE

What purpose is served by our moral judgment of others—and of ourselves? Acknowledging and living out a sense of right and wrong is an expression of our maturity and freedom. We may sometimes find it useful to observe the consequences of choices and actions, both our own and those of others, as we decide how we wish to make future decisions. But habitually judging, adopting a critical stance from which to view all that we and others do, can shrink our spirits.

When we routinely expect the worst, our expectations are often met. When instead we make a practice of opening our hearts with understanding, we will find ourselves and others deserving of respect and compassion. As we sit here now, let's breathe out any rejecting, negative judgments. Let's breathe in acceptance of ourselves and others.

Today, I replace judgments of myself and others with acceptance.

 *July 31*

*There is nothing
ordinary about love.*

MICHAEL KLEIN

Seemingly small acts of love can totally change
our experience of ourselves and others. The light
in a friend's eyes, the grateful word or expression
of someone we've helped, the squeeze of a hand,
the tacitly understood sharing of warmth or excitement—these can sustain us. They give us courage,
energy, and inspiration for whatever we're facing.
Instead of focusing on lack, we can see the wealth
of love in the world and add to it. Whether in friendships, romantic partnerships, or other mutually caring relationships, the feelings of love that build and
deepen in us are miracles.

*Today, I see the love that sustains our lives.
I do one thing to increase it.*

August 1

For if you were by my unkindness shaken,
As I by yours, you've passed a hell of time.

WILLIAM SHAKESPEARE
Sonnet 120

Step Eight suggests that we make a list of all those
we have harmed. Often, someone against whom we
are harboring a resentment is also someone we ourselves have injured. Our words, actions, or attitudes may have provoked him or her to retaliate.
Or perhaps the other person's behavior triggered
our own reaction.

Our perception of the past changes when we're
willing to look at our actions from another person's
point of view. When we actively imagine what it
must feel like to be in someone else's shoes, we begin
to learn compassion. We understand that we, too,
have had an effect on others. We become willing to
consider changing the way we think, feel, and act in
relation to others. We begin looking for opportunities to make restitution where we genuinely owe
it, no matter what the response from others may be.

Today, I make a list of all persons I have harmed
and become willing to make amends to them all.

August 2

Blessed is she whose spirit
you can tell by its ease
was a long time in the making.

ALI LIEBEGOTT

Are we withholding love and approval from ourselves or someone else until a problem is solved or
a character defect weeded out? When we see only
our problems and shortcomings, we may be forgetting that it is the universal human condition to be
imperfect. We are continuously changing and evolving. While we take steps to let go of what hasn't
worked and take actions that reflect our values,
we can also be tolerant of our rate of progress.
Healing and growth take time.

Wherever we are in the process of life, our Higher
Power loves us. We can do no less. We can have patience with our imperfections and those of others,
and envision ourselves as people worthy of love, respect, tenderness, and care. We can accept ourselves
just as we are.

Today, I am at ease with myself.
I am lovable, self-accepting, and whole.

August 3

Anyone with eyes and a brain could see categories breaking down, assumptions rupturing, clear-cut identities going the way of the Berlin Wall.

CAROL QUEEN
AND LAWRENCE SCHIMEL

In the time and place in which we live, what does it mean to identify ourselves as lesbian, gay, bisexual, or transgender—or even to be a woman or a man?

We may not be comfortable trying to fit into one of the classifications that have been constructed for us, even by our allies and peers. In considering our options and those of others, we no longer need to be limited by stereotypes or contribute to clichés. Whatever our gender or sexual preference, we can claim all of ourselves. We can acknowledge our idiosyncratic, individual differences—the ways that our erotic, political, and spiritual imaginations don't neatly fit into readily available categories. We can embrace difference, ours and that of others. We can acknowledge our vulnerablilites and our deep sources of strength. We can tell our own life stories, reveal ourselves in all our complexity, and make ourselves truly known.

Today, I embrace the ways I am different.

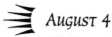

August 4

*Gift, like genius, I often think only means
an infinite capacity for taking pains.*

JANE ELLICE HOPKINS

Each of us has particular talents. It's our responsibility to recognize and honor them. Some of us, having resolved issues of lesbian, gay, bisexual, or transgender orientation, are now becoming aware of other issues. For others, addiction may have prevented us from developing our potential until now. Whether we're becoming aware of what we have to offer or are already on the path of using our gifts, we needn't compare ourselves with others or become discouraged with our rate of progress.

Patience with ourselves and our process and faith and persistence in working toward a goal are attributes that each of us can make his or her own. They increase our confidence and strengthen our willingness to continue setting goals. They deepen our pleasure in the journey itself, whatever time it takes to achieve the outcome.

Today, I take a step toward the realization of my goals.

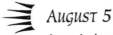 ## August 5

A good education is another name for happiness.
ANN PLATO

Most of us think of education as something attained through schools and degree programs. And, in fact, increased self-esteem and courage have opened many of us to possibilities for furthering our formal education. But healing and spiritual growth are the result of another sort of education that is open to all of us each day. Opportunities to awaken our spirits continue throughout life.

The pain we may have suffered in our families and in society, personal traumas, mistakes we have made, things we may wish we'd done differently— we can put all of these experiences to use. Whatever we have suffered can expand our perspective on human life and increase our usefulness to others. Knowledge of life and overcoming obstacles can make us wiser and more compassionate as community members, mentors, lovers, and friends. We know that the education of our hearts, like that of our minds, takes time and study.

Today, I am grateful for all of my experience.

August 6

*Two may talk together under the same roof
for many years, yet never really meet;
and two others at first speech are old friends.*

MARY CATHERWOOD

However well we think we know the people in our
lives, there is still more to learn. Whether we're
at the beginning or have already participated for
some time in the process of a romantic attachment,
friendship, professional association, or sponsor-
sponsee relationship, we have the opportunity to
achieve greater mutual understanding and connection. Open-mindedness, sincere interest, and the
willingness to be seen and known are essential
ingredients.

We're not required to reveal everything at once
and probably can't. Relationships unfold over time,
through repeated interactions. And the same degree
of intimacy isn't appropriate or possible in all relationships. But what about relationships in which
we continually find ourselves holding back? When
we let go of the fear of looking bad, we no longer
have to hide ourselves and our feelings. We open
doors to being known and accepted as we are. We
must be willing to extend to others the same opportunity for openness. When we suspend judgment
and offer others genuine attention, warmth, and
understanding, new and old relationships develop
in unexpected ways.

Today, I learn something new in a relationship.

August 7

For my survivor lover
pain has no boundaries
spills to our howling bed

ELIZABETH LORDE-ROLLINS

The love we offer others, important as it is, cannot heal all wounds. Those we're close to may suffer from past violence, abuse, or other traumatic experiences. Or they may be recovering from addictions. Anger, pain, or grief may surface as they heal and rebuild a sense of self. They may suffer at times from self-doubt and low self-esteem. We must understand that as those we love reclaim themselves, their ups and downs will affect our interactions. We may inadvertently be treated as stand-ins for parents or others from the past; we may sometimes be targets of blame and anger.

It is not our place to analyze or fix another's pain or to give unwanted advice about which therapeutic or recovery program to turn to. But we can assure others of our love and loyalty, giving them room to find the healing path that is appropriate for them. We can refrain from obsessive involvement with another's problems, find support for ourselves, and let fresh air into our own lives. Healing takes time.

Today, I trust the process of my own and others' healing.

 *August 8*

*There are a lot of healing men. . . . Even though
I don't have them in my life the way straight
women do, I have them as friends.*

CHERYL
a lesbian in recovery

Rich, nurturing friendships can and do exist among
many of us and with those whose gender or sexual
identification differs from ours. Relationships with
people with whom we once thought it unlikely to
experience closeness may in fact be especially healing. Such friendships are free from the tensions of
romantic relationships. They can give us a safe context in which to repair the past, to experience intimacy, to play, to grow, to cultivate our ability to
communicate, and to expand our understanding
and respect for others and ourselves.

We must not perpetuate old, limiting ideas of
who should talk with whom. We have so much
experience, energy, and love to offer one another.
Let's not deprive ourselves or others of the healing
that comes from knowing one another and allowing ourselves to be known.

Today, I expand the possibilities of friendship in my life.

 *August* 9

It is a spiritual axiom that every time we are disturbed, no matter what the cause, there is something wrong with us.

BILL WILSON
cofounder of Alcoholics Anonymous

Aren't others ever to blame for the discomfort in which we find ourselves? Many of us find ourselves thinking, "How could my friend do this to me? And after all I've done for her!" Our anger and righteous indignation seem justified, too, when the forces of law, politics, or society perpetrate an injustice that affects the lives of gay, lesbian, bisexual, and transgender people. But blaming others and clinging to a sense of victimization does not bring healing, empowerment, or true change. Only taking responsibility for our attitudes, feelings, and actions can accomplish that.

We cannot directly change other people or institutions and we cannot be certain that our actions will achieve the outcomes we desire. Nevertheless, we *can* choose not to remain in states of passivity or victimization. The actions we take toward change, even small actions, increase our energy and have an energizing effect on those around us. While we cannot guarantee outcomes, an attitude of responsibility releases us from the syndrome of blaming and victimhood. It is freedom.

Today, I take responsibility for my attitudes and actions.

August 10

Have nothing in your houses that you do not know to be useful, or believe to be beautiful.

WILLIAM MORRIS

When our homes and other environments in which we spend time reflect our sense of beauty and harmony, we feel pleasure and peacefulness. Similarly, when our actions and our connections with others embody our best sense of ourselves, our day is a source of satisfaction and serenity.

Just as we can eliminate clothes we no longer wear from our closets and objects from our homes that no longer reflect who we are, we can let go of behaviors and attitudes that no longer serve the needs of our spirit. Housecleaning, whether literal or figurative, comes from a state of mind that is willing to let go. The past is past. We can make room for the ways that we are healing, growing, and changing. Instead of dreading to let go of what is no longer beautiful, we can feel exhilaration. We are clearing a space for the unexpected.

Today, I let go of the past and make room for new and unexpected beauty in my life.

August 11

*Withdrawal from the world is something we can,
and perhaps should, do every day. It completes
the movement of which entering fully into life
is only one part.*

THOMAS MOORE

In a piece of music or poetry, there are pauses,
places of rest and stillness for the ear or eye. They
help us absorb and integrate what has come before
and prepare us to receive what will follow. Such
places of stillness in a work of art can convey powerful emotion more effectively than a nonstop suc-
cession of words or images. Silent meditation, too,
can calm us or fill us with a sense of awe, can help
us connect with Spirit as effectively as the words
of prayer. Moments of quiet shared at a recovery
meeting or with another person can produce
a tangible feeling of communication and oneness.

   We need not fear stillness. It is not the silence
of self-censorship. Instead, let's look for the places
where quiet resides deep within us and in the natural world. Let's deliberately turn to those places for
rest and refreshment. Let's renew our sense of self-
hood and purpose, undistracted by the conflict and
clamor of others' demands and of our own stream
of thoughts. In the depths of stillness, we can find
our own voice.

Today, I create the quiet that nurtures me.

August 12

I make
This vow to never squander me again
DENTON WELCH

We may have struggled to understand and accept our identities, whether as gay, lesbian, bisexual, or transgender people or as people recovering from addictions. For many, clearing away what is no longer relevant to our lives has been a source of energy and freedom. Even experiences of loss and the deaths of loved ones serve us as a reminder that our lives are precious and our time is not infinite. As a result of our experience, we have begun to see more clearly what our purpose is at this time of our lives.

Knowing ourselves goes hand in hand with a commitment to use what we know. If we want to work in a particular area, we need to prepare actively and reach out to the world we want to take part in. If we need healing from addiction, we can choose a program of recovery and take the suggested Steps. To achieve our goals and maintain success as we've defined it, we must stay on target and not waste our life force on what we know is unworthy of our commitment.

Today, I invest my energy in what I value most.

# AugUST 13

And I ask you: well, what are we going to do about it?

JUNE JORDAN

As gay, lesbian, bisexual, or transgender people, we have a finely tuned sense of justice. Many of us love to express our opinions on what's wrong with the world and on what others should or shouldn't have said or done. Some of us are cynical about the future and habitually predict troubled encounters with mainstream society. Perhaps we're fond of blaming "the system," expert at analyzing its flaws and its negative impact on us.

Passivity combined with negative judgment is a deadly partnership. It kills spirit, initiative, and hope. Instead, we must cultivate a sense that the actions we take matter. Even seemingly small gestures—praising a new idea, thanking another person for honest sharing, making a brief phone call of appreciation or connection—can set in motion a process that works to create new projects, ends a sense of isolation or unworthiness, even saves lives. History has shown that dedicated individuals and small groups working together can make an enormous difference. Things can change direction in a day. And we ourselves are changed through taking actions that honor our beliefs.

Today, I put a belief into action.

August 14

Dysfunctional homes do not just happen. They are created by parents who themselves were not adequately taken care of and nurtured.

TIAN DAYTON

We have opportunities in our lives to end the cycle of dysfunction that successive generations inherit. As gay, lesbian, bisexual, and transgender people, we have had the courage to define ourselves differently from our families. Those of us who embrace recovery, too, embark on a path that offers freedom from addiction, freedom from continuing to repeat past mistakes, and a chance to restore wholeness, hope, and joy.

While extricating ourselves from family patterns is challenging, it is possible. Therapeutic counseling, support networks, and recovery programs are among our available resources. Accepting and facing the legacy of family problems—alcoholism, workaholism, violence, abuse—can strengthen us. Identifying family traditions and patterns such as enmeshment, underachievement, or overresponsibility frees us and increases our options. We don't have to reject our families of origin. Understanding what shaped them can increase our compassion and our ability to detach with love as we gently nurture ourselves.

Today, I see my family clearly. I lovingly detach from patterns that no longer work for the good in my life.

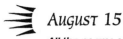

August 15

All the poems of our lives are not yet made.

MURIEL RUKEYSER

We can point to signs of progress in the evolution of our healing and maturing. We have taken steps in developing our relationships with ourselves, other people, and Spirit. We have begun to accept and forgive ourselves and others. We have welcomed fresh ideas about our identities and possibilities for growth. Whether gradually or suddenly, we have let in new attitudes and begun to cultivate new habits. New selves are continuously evolving out of the old as we become free of what is no longer true for us.

Conscious awareness of how much we have changed over time can give us hope for our future. We can look forward expectantly for more good to enter our lives. We can make worthy commitments, so that we ourselves have a hand in gently guiding our transformation into the people we wish to become.

Today, I commit myself to healing transformation.

 **AugUST 16**

With rue my heart is laden
For golden friends I had.

A. E. HOUSMAN

Perhaps a close friend or peer has died, perhaps we've lost a mentor or valuable teacher, or perhaps a relationship has ended. Our first responses may include anger, sorrow, discouragement, or fear at having to go on without someone who gave meaning to our lives. It takes time to acknowledge and release these feelings of despair. They are an inevitable and necessary part of the universal mourning process.

No one remains with us permanently. Some people are with us for a long time, others for a brief, significant moment. It is a blessing to have someone's company for a part of our journey. In time, as we give expression to our feelings of loss, we move to another stage of the process. We begin to see what gifts particular people have given us, how we have been enlivened or strengthened by their approach to life, and what qualities of theirs we have made our own. The impact that others have had on us need not be lost. They live on in our appreciation of the ways they have changed us.

Today, I am grateful for the gift of another's presence on part of my journey.

August 17

I live in constant negotiations
trying to resolve
the border conflicts raging inside me

JUDIT
a Jewish-Argentinean lesbian

Identity is rarely a simple matter. If we take the risk
of truly knowing ourselves, we will probably have
to face complexity and inner conflict. We may feel
pulled in one direction by the values of our families
of origin or the traditions of a religion in which
we were raised, pulled in another direction by the
culture and commitments of our communities, and
pulled yet again by the ways that we sense ourselves
to be different from any of these.

Each of us is an original combination of influ-
ences and desires, conformities and revolutions.
We must give ourselves permission to be the rich,
complex people we are. When we acknowledge
and embrace our conflicts rather than rushing to
eliminate them through denial, we become freer
to choose how we wish to respond to the situations
in our lives.

Today, I value and embrace my individuality
in all its complexity.

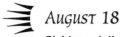 *August 18*

*Right now is the time to wake up from your
sleepwalking through this life.*

MEL ASH

Some of us go through each day passively, as if we
had no control over the direction of our experiences.
We may think that luck or the actions of others are
responsible for all that occurs. In fact, we have
many choices. Awareness of our opportunities to
choose and our use of that freedom are significant
factors in shaping each day.

We can look searchingly at where we are and
what we've contributed to our present situation.
We can acknowledge and accept with compassion
whoever we have been and whatever we have done
in the past. We can empower ourselves to decide
which attitudes and behaviors we would like to embrace and continue and which we'd like to change.
We need not be stuck in passivity. We can choose
new directions that foster healing and growth.

*Today, I take actions that invite healing
and positive change into my life.*

 Augus⊤ 19

Adversity forces the gay man to develop a creative genius for living.

STANLEY SIEGEL

We may wish to work toward changing some aspects of our circumstances. We may not wish to repeat our past mistakes. But whatever our desires for change, we can be grateful for all of our experiences as gay, lesbian, bisexual, and transgender people.

In the midst of an inhospitable culture, we've arrived at an understanding of who we are and have created our own supportive communities. Having experienced ourselves as outsiders, we've developed a gift for working "outside the lines." We are not afraid of originality, creativity, or independence from convention and tradition. Some part of us knows we can make our way, mapping our course as we go along, thriving even under adverse conditions.

Everything that occurred in the past can be useful to us today. We can make more informed choices. We can develop our understanding of how changes take place over time. We can view ourselves and others with compassion and a sense of humor. We can cultivate faith that the Spirit that has brought us to this day continues in our lives as a source of inspiration and joy.

Today, I value everything that has occurred in my life so far.

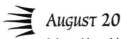 *August 20*

I do not love him because he is good,
but because he is my little child.

RABINDRANATH TAGORE

What is it that makes us feel love for another person? Do we love those who follow the rules, make no mistakes, and do everything we think they should? In fact, love for others springs up in us independent of others' goodness. We love others freely, and we would be hard put to give our reasons. Those of us who have children in our lives know how little our feelings of love for them have to do with their goodness. At the sight of a child's innocence and vulnerability, our hearts simply open.

We can love others and ourselves the same way we love children—tenderly and unconditionally. This is the way our Higher Power loves us. If we are struggling with acceptance of ourselves, we can envision the attitude of a loving, nurturing parent. Instead of yelling, "Stop that!" or "You're bad!" the loving parent within us can take us gently by the hand and lead us in a new direction. Whatever our mistakes or rate of progress, our loving inner parents need never withhold love.

Today, I offer myself the acceptance and
unconditional love that I would offer a child.

AUGUST 21

Love between women is seen as a paradigm of love between equals, and that is perhaps its greatest attraction.

ELIZABETH JANEWAY

In our relationships with other lesbian, gay, bisexual, or transgender people, we may at times be tempted to perpetuate old feelings and attitudes of powerlessness and inequality. We may deny ourselves or others full status in a relationship, perpetuating a notion that one or the other of us has more value.

Each of us has unique gifts, knowledge, and experience to contribute to any relationship. This does not make us greater than others in our lives. Each of us has flaws and foibles. This doesn't give us less dignity or worth than others. The world around us offers numerous examples of relationships in which there is an imbalance—and frequently abuse—of power. Rather than perpetuate such inequality in our lives, we can cultivate respect for the worth, dignity, and wholeness of others and ourselves.

Today, I foster a sense of equality with other people.

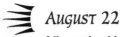 *August 22*

Mirrors should reflect a little before throwing back images.

JEAN COCTEAU

What forms our images of ourselves? Perhaps we have been quick to judge, continuing to evaluate ourselves on the basis of criticisms we received as children or of values perpetuated by mainstream culture. Or perhaps we've looked at ourselves through eyes of denial, not seeing where we have the need and ability to take steps to develop and heal our lives.

Our self-images have power. What we believe about ourselves and our capacity for change creates the attitude and posture we show the rest of the world. When we view ourselves negatively, without kindness or compassion, we present a clouded face to others—and they reflect it back to us. When we view ourselves with humor, gentleness, and hope, we present a positive image that shows others how to regard us. And like others, we tend to believe the self-images we create and respond to ourselves accordingly. We can have a powerful impact on our experiences each day by creating positive images of ourselves.

Today, I see myself as worthy of love and respect. Wherever I go, my positive self-image brings light.

August 23

Recovery is not a perfect picture. It's a human experience that has moments of perfection.

MARY BOYLE

Addictions to chemical substances and destructive behaviors have long been prevalent in our gay, lesbian, bisexual, and transgender communities. What may have started as recreation, a desire to connect, or a way to cope with painful experience can rebound, replacing momentary comfort or connection with pain and isolation. What may have begun as a survival strategy now threatens our health, perhaps even our lives.

Even when our denial of the seriousness of addictive habits is punctured, some of us would go to great lengths to avoid entering a Twelve Step program. Some of us imagine recovery as restrictive and repressive. In fact, the opposite is true. Recovery can help us be true to our individual and idiosyncratic desires. We may not agree with or like everyone we meet in recovery. We may not wish to follow every suggestion recovery offers us. The healing we experience will probably come gradually rather than instantaneously. But we *will* experience healing if we are open to it. Recognizing and treating addiction is necessary if we are to flourish as creative, independent, and courageous members of our communities.

Today, I look honestly at the impact of addictive habits. I keep an open mind about recovery.

August 24

Only connect! . . . Live in fragments no longer.
Only connect, and the beast and the monk,
robbed of the isolation that is life to either, will die.

E. M. FORSTER

The health of the human family requires that we connect with one another. It requires, too, that we each integrate the different aspects of ourselves. Our spirits don't flourish through rejecting our bodies and denying their needs and wants. And our bodies, including their desire for sexual expression, are part of a larger picture that includes thoughts, emotions, and spiritual experience. We cannot accept the view that bisexual, transgender, lesbian, and gay people should deny their sexual or gender identity to be integrated into the human family. Nor can we accept that we are driven exclusively by the physical or that spirituality belongs only to those who deny the body.

Our lives are physical, mental, and spiritual. We are whole people. If we are to be healthy and whole, all aspects of us require expression and integration. We can look searchingly at our lives to see which circumstances foster a sense of wholeness, which a sense of fragmentation. We can look at which needs are being exalted at the expense of others. We can bring spiritual awareness to physical experience and ground our spiritual perceptions in what our bodies tell us.

Today, I am one person, aware of my whole self—
physical, mental, and spiritual—in each experience.

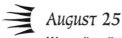 *August 25*

*We can't really forgive another until first
we have forgiven ourselves.*

TIAN DAYTON

Forgiveness is not merely something that occurs in
one dramatic moment, ending long enmity or separation. Forgiveness is a state of mind we can cultivate each day to clarify, enliven, and sustain our
relationships to one another and ourselves.

Self-forgiveness, far more effectively than self-
punishment, allows us to change. When we forgive
ourselves for actions we may have taken or been
unable to take in the past, our spirits lighten.
Without focusing on shame or guilt, we're freer
to choose new approaches and make amends by
truly changing some of the ways we relate to others. And when we don't harbor grievances, but instead acknowledge our feelings honestly and let
go of them quickly, we walk through the day without the heavy burden of resentment.

A forgiving state of mind produces healing in
our torn connections with ourselves, other people,
and our Higher Power. It increases a sense of our
worth and the worth of others. It opens the door to
lightness and joyfulness. It nourishes love. It makes
room for the new.

Today, I keep forgiveness in my heart and mind.

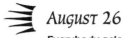 AUGUST 26

*Everybody gets so much information all day long
that they lose their common sense.*

GERTRUDE STEIN

We are bombarded daily by images and words that
claim our attention. Much of this barrage comes
from mainstream media, but much also comes from
our communities. How are we to sort through all
this information and decide what truly deserves our
attention? How do we keep from being pulled in
myriad directions?

There are ways we can come back to our center
and listen to the Spirit that moves us. One is to attend a daily meeting of a recovery program. Others'
stories of choosing life over death, of the loving
guidance of a Higher Power, and of working the suggested Steps are powerful reminders of our primary
purpose. Another is to read literature that reminds
us of our spiritual essence and offers us an affirmation we can return to for inspiration throughout the
day. Still another is to take time apart from the noise
and confusion of the day, contemplating art or nature or refreshing ourselves with prayer or meditation. It's not only possible but essential that we stand
back from the fray—inner or outer—and remind
ourselves of who we are and why we are here.

Today, I seek moments of stillness.

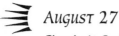 *August 27*

Glory be to God for dappled things—

. . . .

All things counter, original, spare, strange.

GERARD MANLEY HOPKINS

Are we still trying to fit in, whether in the larger society or the culture of our own communities? Are we rejecting ourselves because we haven't found a vital part of ourselves reflected in the institutions, programs, arts, and literature either of the mainstream or of gay, lesbian, bisexual, and transgender life?

Instead of looking at our differences as liabilities, let's embrace them as our uniqueness and strength. When we claim ourselves, we give permission to others to claim themselves as well. The more of us who speak up honestly, the less isolated we are. The less rejecting of ourselves we are, the less others will respond to us with rejection.

Each of us is part of the glory of creation. Let's declare our understanding of our unique identities with confidence. It is a service to ourselves and others. It is a delight to our Higher Power.

Today, I claim part of myself that I have rejected.

*Courage is resistance to fear, mastery of fear—
not absence of fear.*

MARK TWAIN

The words *courage* and *daring* mean different things
to each of us. For some of us, coming out to family
or peers as gay, lesbian, bisexual, or transgender
people requires daring. For others, becoming entirely honest about addictive behavior seems full
of risk. Over time, the various meanings of courage
may change for each of us, depending upon what
challenges us at different moments. Something
we've experienced as threatening in the past may
come easily to us now that it's no longer unknown
territory.

   Each day offers opportunities to experience our
capacity for courage as we face new experiences
and unforeseeable outcomes. We are offered opportunities, too, to trust that we will not be given more
than we can handle on any day. We have the chance
to remember that we are loved and supported by
friends, community, and a loving Higher Power.
We can replace fear with faith. We are not alone.

Today, I take an action that requires courage.

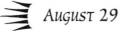 AUGUST 29

*You never know what is enough until you know
what is more than enough.*

WILLIAM BLAKE

Most of us recognize when we've gone beyond simply meeting a need and have reached the point of
excess. The healthy response is to stop when we've
had enough, whether of food, exercise, sex, work—
or even of trying to help others. Compulsion means
having difficulty knowing what our own limits are,
being unable to stop when body, mind, and emotions tell us to stop.

Far more satisfying than having too much of
anything is the experience of knowing who we are,
accepting the need for boundaries, becoming willing to ask our Higher Power for help in meeting our
needs appropriately, and helping others through
sharing our experience of overcoming compulsion.
When we are willing to acknowledge a compulsion
and ask for help, we experience the presence of
Spirit in our lives. Feelings of isolation and deprivation are replaced by a deep sense of connection and
fullness.

Today, I am enough, I have enough, I do enough.

August 30

Yesternight the sun went hence,
And yet is here today.

JOHN DONNE

Is life an endless series of problems? When we hear another person reciting a litany of complaints or troubles or obsessively going over the details of a particular difficulty, we know that problems give a far from complete picture of life's possibilities. We can easily see another's temporary loss of perspective. We may try reminding a friend that he or she has come through difficulties in the past and that there is hope for the future.

We can be a friend to ourselves, too, by remembering, when we are in the midst of obsession or negative thinking, that we don't have the complete picture. We have survived past difficulties. We do not know what the future will bring. We can use meditation or prayer to broaden our perspective to include our Higher Power. The Serenity Prayer can help us to relax and breathe:

God grant us the serenity
To accept the things we cannot change,
Courage to change the things we can,
And wisdom to know the difference.

Today, I use the Serenity Prayer
to change my perspective.

 *August 31*

*In either case, passing as "straight" or passing
for white, the "passing" person must accept
the twin albatross of silence and invisibility.*

CHERYL CLARKE

Some of us are visible and active in lesbian, gay,
bisexual, and transgender communities. Many are
"out" in our transactions with other communities as
well. Whatever the extent of our visibility, perhaps
there are still situations in which we believe it easier
for us to keep silent. But when we impose silence
and invisibility on ourselves, thinking it will be easier, we in fact drain our psychic energy. Whether we
choose to "pass" or believe that "passing" has been
imposed on us by circumstances, some part of us
remains preoccupied with fear and secrecy.

Seeking employment or housing, attending a
social gathering, or conversing with a neighbor—
we sense different degrees of risk in a variety of situations. We can begin to notice whether we feel the
impulse to say nothing when someone assumes that
our sexuality or gender identity conforms to their
expectations. Most of us can acknowledge our identities in a broader spectrum of situations than we
have previously thought safe. When silence and
invisibility are lifted, we connect more completely
with others, with Spirit, and with ourselves.

*Today, I free myself in some small way
from the baggage of silence and invisibility.*

September 1

Good judgment, a careful sense of timing, courage, and prudence—these are the qualities we shall need when we take Step Nine.

Twelve Steps and Twelve Traditions

Sometimes we feel such eagerness to rid ourselves of guilt or other uncomfortable feelings that we don't consider the possible consequences of blurting out the truth. Step Nine, while suggesting that we make amends to those we've harmed, reminds us to refrain from injuring others. While not procrastinating out of fear or pride, we must consider how our words and the way we speak them will affect others' welfare and self-esteem.

When we commit ourselves to fundamental change, such as recovery from addictive substances or behaviors, we may rush to tell others that they can expect to see a major turnaround in our manner of living. But changes in our attitudes and actions are needed to prepare the way for a spoken apology—and sometimes may even take its place. The purpose of making amends is to heal the way we live in this world with others. Even when someone isn't ready to accept our amends, our honesty and genuine effort to act differently change us in profoundly positive ways.

Today, I make amends with sincerity and care.

September 2

In Falls, North Carolina, in 1957, we had just one way of "coming out." It was called getting caught.

ALAN GURGANUS

Thanks to generations of work by gay, lesbian, bisexual, and transgender activists and to the continuing evolution of tolerance in the world, claiming our identity is no longer a crime. While there is still more work to do before the human family acknowledges and includes all of its children, encouraging progress has been made.

We can help sustain and increase freedom in the world by maintaining freedom within ourselves. We need not turn our spirits over to feelings of guilt and shame about a nonconforming sexual or gender identity. We need not internalize the lie of any sort of prejudice. Our Higher Power loves us as we are, without reservation. We must do no less. Our complete self-acceptance, including love for the gift of our sexuality, is a way of loving and honoring our Higher Power.

Today, I am free of any reservations about who I am.

September 3

Meditation is not a way to enlightenment, nor is it a method of achieving anything at all. It is peace and blessedness itself. It is the actualization of wisdom, the ultimate truth of the oneness of all things.

DOGEN
translated by Stephen Mitchell

Meditation need not be limited to time spent sitting with our eyes closed. We can practice a type of meditation simply in the way we live our lives each day.

Often, we think about our lives in terms of what we hope to accomplish, but in truth, we don't always have to aim at goals or results. Whatever we are engaged in doing throughout our day, we can cherish the experience of simply being alive and sensing our connection with everything else that is alive. We can remember our unity with others and with Spirit. When we stop focusing on a destination we are striving to reach and instead focus on the present moment in all its fullness, we experience aliveness without struggle and enjoy a deep sense of calm. Paradoxically, when we stop concentrating on effort and relax into being present, giving whatever we are doing all our attention, we find ourselves accomplishing our goals with greater ease.

Today, I relax into being alive in each moment.

September 4

I suppose everything is finally instructive,
and that every lover is a kind of teacher.

CARL PHILLIPS

Relationships don't just happen to us. At times in
our process of growth, we choose to enter or
deepen connections to others. We find ourselves
willing to be more open, both to those new to us
and to those with whom we're already engaged in
relationships. We open up to others with hope and
faith that they will answer our longings.

When our needs for connection and communication are being met, we learn about our capacity to
choose appropriately, to be present and loving, and
to find satisfaction in relationships. When relationships backfire or fizzle, there is also much to learn.
Loves and friendships that have ended teach us
about our needs and boundaries, what expectations
are realistic, what attitudes and patterns we bring to
relationships, and where our beliefs need to evolve.
Endings are not necessarily failures. We can value
all of our experiences as they teach us—sometimes
through comfort, sometimes through discomfort—
who we are and how we wish to relate to others.

Today, I look at the pattern of my relationships to see
what I want to keep and what I want to heal and change.

September 5

When Colleen first came to live with me, my son drew a picture of her with a beard. Even though we were securely closeted, he knew. When he graduated from high school, he invited Colleen. He said that our being lesbians had opened doors for him, that he was able to have a more expanded view of life's possibilities.

MARCIA SCHWEMER

Instead of merely hoping for tolerance of our loving relationships, believing that we shouldn't upset the status quo or create problems for our children, families of origin, or friends, we can begin to view ourselves and our relationships as a force for positive change in the world. When we know who we are and live our gay, lesbian, bi-sexual, or transgender lives without apology or shame, we serve as powerful examples. We help to strengthen tolerance for difference. We offer others—both adults and children—permission to be themselves. We expand the meanings of love, courage, loyalty, self-expression, and nurturing. We can trust that our originality and bravery in creating new forms of family is furthering con-sciousness and healing in the world.

Today, my self-acceptance is a powerful example to others.

September 6

*This is where I yank the old roots
from my chest, like the tomatoes
we let grow until December, stalks
thick as saplings.*

ELLEN BASS

What are the habits or attitudes we've let run wild
in us? Which old loyalties and attachments have
lost their vitality? We can be like gardeners as we
take an honest look at what needs changing in our
lives. There are opportune moments for facing and
rooting out what we've neglected in the past. When
we are ready, we can pull up the roots of the old
without a struggle.

Sometimes, new growth comes with surprising
speed and abundance when we have had the courage
to let go of what is no longer alive for us. Our past
can become part of our spiritual "compost heap" in
which nothing is wasted. What we remember and
understand of our past experiences will help us to
flourish in seasons to come.

*Today, I look at my life like a gardener, recognizing
what needs to be uprooted, what needs protection
from the cold, and what needs fertilizing.*

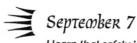

September 7

I learn that safety is where we make it

EKUA OMOSUPE

We each have different images of safety. Some associate safety with having a secure job, enough money (however we define "enough"), a home of our own, or a partner willing to stick by us forever. Some think safety comes with being given a clean bill of health by a physician. But not everyone who has these things feels truly secure, and many who lack them walk fearlessly through their days.

Material comfort, physical health, promises— there is no guarantee that any of these will bless us permanently. A true, lasting sense of safety lies elsewhere. We are safe when we know so well who we are that no one can dissuade us from our self-knowledge. We are safe when we decide to trust the love our Higher Power has for us. We are safe when we are more concerned with how we can serve others than with what they can do for us or take from us.

Safety comes from having an open mind, a generous heart, and a resilient spirit.

Today, my knowledge and acceptance of who I am and my deepening relationship with a Higher Power give me a feeling of security.

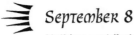

September 8

*Nothing contributes so much to tranquilize
the mind as a steady purpose.*

MARY WOLLSTONECRAFT

Each of us must choose priorities in our lives—
priorities for which we work and live. If we stay
focused on our highest priority for today, then we
won't be pulled this way and that by such inner or
outer distractions as others' wants and opinions
or the temptation to measure our supposed success
or failure at every step of our journey.

We need not "take our own pulse" constantly.
We can enjoy the experience of each moment, relax-
ing in the knowledge of how to handle any conflict
that arises. Having clearly stated to ourselves what
our central purpose is, we have a map. When we are
uncertain about whether or not to take a particular
action, we can ask ourselves whether taking it will
bring us closer to or further from our goals.

*Today, I know what my priorities are
and I state them clearly.*

September 9

When you are openly gay in Korea, your family declares you dead and holds a funeral for you. The family book lists you as deceased. Prayers are said for you once a year at the family shrine and incense is burned for your ghost.

ALEX CHEE

According to some families and community members, our gay, lesbian, bisexual, and transgender lives are not lives at all. But rejection by others cannot erase us. It is only when we conspire with others to reject ourselves that rejection can harm us.

Let us take special care to cherish ourselves, treating ourselves with gentleness and tenderness, as we would treat a child entrusted to our care. Let's view our needs with respect, paying special attention to whatever ways our bodies and spirits require nurturing. Let's breathe out critical, negative ideas and breathe in complete acceptance of ourselves. Let's grant ourselves and one another full status as members of the human family.

Today, I offer myself acceptance, kindness, and loving care. I join with those who honor my existence as I honor theirs.

September 10

I have an inalienable right to love whom I may, to love for as long or as short a period as I can, and to change that love every day if I please!

VICTORIA WOODHULL

Many of us are just beginning to learn that we can allow time for loving relationships to develop, that we needn't discard someone the moment the road seems bumpy. Changing our love each day, to which suffragette Victoria Woodhull proclaimed her right in 1871, may sound to us like an affirmation of frivolousness or a call to instability. But Woodhull made her extravagant statement at a time when women had few options outside of traditional marriage. Exaggeration can be a striking way to make a point.

We need not let society, family, or even those in our gay, lesbian, bisexual, and transgender communities dictate to us whom it is appropriate to love or what form love should take. We need to learn to listen to our deep, inner sense of what is right for us. We live in a time that offers us the option of being true to ourselves. Following inner guidance rather than convention, we can make relationship choices that are uniquely appropriate and that support our lives.

Today, love is my choice, not my duty.

September 11

Once we recognize what it is we are feeling, we recognize we can feel deeply, love deeply, can feel joy, then we will demand that all parts of our lives produce that kind of joy.

AUDRE LORDE

When we deny our feelings, even in some small way, we deaden ourselves and our experience of the moment; we cut off our channel of communication with a Higher Power. We frustrate truth and stop the flow of change in us and around us.

When we have the willingness to be fully alive, fully in touch, aware of all that we're feeling—even feelings to which we've assigned a negative value—joy can enter. Our bodies and souls hum with the vibration of a universe large enough to hold us, large enough to hold all that breathes. We are free from hiding and holding ourselves in check. We are free from having to judge one feeling "good," another "bad." We are free from isolation. We no longer feel cut off from Spirit. In fact, we recognize that Spirit is everywhere: in ourselves, in other people, in nature. Joy is a dance that the entire universe is engaged in, and we can join the dance.

Today, I drink deeply of the joy of being alive.

September 12

When we learn what a relationship can give us, and what is unfair or inappropriate to expect of one another, we are free to go about our personal development with the loving support of partners.

TIAN DAYTON

When we have expected others to fill the empty spaces in us, we have usually been disappointed. It is our very sense of *who we are* that draws people to us.

We have the power to fulfill ourselves with what is available to us. We have a choice at all times. If we are obsessed with a person or incident, we can make the choice to let go. We can talk tenderly to ourselves. We can nurture and develop ourselves with music, exercise, writing therapy, Twelve Step meetings, or meditation. We can offer service to our communities. Whether or not we are participating in a romantic relationship, our comfort and our identities are our own responsibilities.

Today, I take responsibility for my happiness.

September 13

Slowly I find myself being weaned from her material presence. Yet filled with her as never before. . . . She gave me love, to love myself, and to love the world. I must remember how to love.

TOBY TALBOT

The loss of a parent, partner, close friend, or community member through death or separation happens to each of us in time. Among some lesbian, gay, bisexual, and transgender people, to have experienced such loss is more the rule than the exception. Of course, death and loss are endings. But they can be significant beginnings, too.

The loss of one close to us seems to make us more aware than ever of a loved person's qualities of mind and spirit: kindness, a sense of humor, or depth of commitment. When we remember loved attributes of an absent friend, we say that he or she "lives on in us." We emulate characteristics that we miss in order to do honor to someone's memory. Those we have lost have taught us well. We begin to embody their attributes in ourselves. Whatever else, loss of a loved one teaches and deepens our ability to value and love one another.

Today, I remember how to love.

September 14

No one should have to live in shadows, I told myself. From an early age I had been taught that discrimination was wrong. Yet here I was, a homosexual man, discriminating against myself, as if I were the agent of my society.

CHARLES SILVERSTEIN

Within the gay, lesbian, bisexual, and transgender communities, we often speak of oppression of those like us by the people and institutions of society at large. We speak less often of our own internalization of society's values, especially of its discriminatory attitudes and policies.

We can root out any of the ways that we discriminate against ourselves in attitude, word, or action, and make room for the tender beginnings of a new relationship with ourselves. In this new relationship, respect and courtesy prevail. Instead of raging at ourselves or engaging in a battle with habits and feelings that are no longer useful, we ask ourselves what need or purpose these habits and feelings may have served. Lovingly, we release them. Gradually, our relationship with ourselves becomes more open and positive.

Today, I lovingly release thoughts and actions that are in any way discriminatory.

September 15

*God wants nothing of you but the gift
of a peaceful heart.*

MEISTER ECKHART

The ability to keep peace within us is indeed a gift.
We can cultivate the art of keeping peace in our
hearts despite problems or challenges we encounter,
despite others' words or actions.

One path to peace is remembering the difference
between things we can and can't control. When we
take actions that are appropriate in a given circumstance and let go of trying to predict or control
their outcome, we will have mastered a major challenge to maintaining a peaceful way of life. Another path to peace is not to blame people or events
for our negative feelings and attitudes, but instead
to be willing to look at what we ourselves may
have contributed to creating our own discomfort.

We don't have to be saints to create peace in our
hearts. At any time during the day, we can step back
from conflict within us or around us and breathe
slowly, rhythmically, and deeply. We will be surprised at the calm that soon reenters our thoughts
and visions of the world. Our serenity will help
others to find the reservoir of peace in their hearts.

Today, let peace on earth begin with my peaceful heart.

September 16

*If I try to look for the goodness in people,
and even active drunks have goodness
in them, then I'd say living isn't so bad.*

KATIE
a recovering alcoholic

We can choose to be active in creating positive and
loving connections with our fellow human beings
rather than passively waiting for others to conquer
their character defects and behave more as we wish
them to.

There is good in the worst of us. When we are
having difficulty appreciating or communicating
with someone, we can ask our Higher Power to
help us see what is good and worthwhile in that
person. We can view her or him with compassion,
knowing that circumstances beyond our control
help to shape human lives, knowing that spiritual
deprivation and hunger are at the root of many
attitudes and behaviors we wish were different.
We can pray sincerely for a person's complete well-
being, visualizing her or him as thriving, whole,
and happy. As we take these steps, we will find our
hearts opening. Often, others will reflect our attitude of love and forgiveness. Our sense of others
will be generous, and our own spirits will be lifted.

Today, I look for the goodness in others.

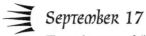

September 17

The real voyage of discovery consists not in seeking new landscapes but in having new eyes.

MARCEL PROUST

What aspect of our lives today would change radically if we could change our thinking? Perhaps we feel confined by a limitation we've imposed on ourselves: "That's not something I could learn to do," "No one in my family has ever . . . ," "I'm too old," or simply "I'm not good enough." Perhaps we've repeated ideas of limitation so often that we truly believe them. Our beliefs shape our possibilities; they can close doors to us, and they can open them.

Beliefs are capable of change. Let's take an honest look at one of the ways that we have confined the scope of our lives through a limiting belief. Just for today, let's affirm that we have the ability to change. Let's notice and appreciate the energy that accompanies our statement of a new, positive belief. Let's think of a single step we can take that expresses our change of vision.

Today, I let go of one limiting attitude. I take a step toward expanding my sense of my life's possibilities.

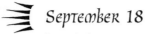

September 18

I married as a means of erasing
homosexual desire.

CARL PHILLIPS

Have we been false to our deepest desires, betraying ourselves, others, or a Higher Power by ignoring the messages that come from our spirit within? If we can identify the ways that we have not been true to ourselves, we can also change them: in the process of transformation, awareness comes first, then compassion and self-acceptance, then new action.

As we review and repair the past, we needn't see our behavior only in black and white. We needn't pass judgment on ways that we have not fully honored desires that come from our deepest selves. Instead, we can look at the ways we *have* recognized and acknowledged our desires. We can make a list of times when we listened to the positive promptings within us, of permissions we gave ourselves to be fully ourselves. We can affirm that we are engaged in an ongoing process of healing, growth, and change.

Today, I take a positive inventory, listing the ways
I have honored my desires for healing and growth.

September 19

*When they ask me, "Did you come to this country
in your astral body?" I say, "Air India actually . . .
pleasant flight."*

EKNATH EASWARAN

Some of us say, "I'm going to get into spirituality
one of these days," thinking of a spiritual path as
something apart from everyday life, when in fact
a spiritual path does not require visions or occult
powers.

Our spirits are not something exotic and apart
from us. When we are kind and loving to our fellow human beings, when we are honest about our
shortcomings, when we ask for help in surrendering addictive behaviors, when we sense our deep
connection with other people—any of these are
ways of making spiritual progress. A spiritual path
is something we can follow in our everyday life.
Amid the noise and problems of an ordinary day
our spirits are challenged to awaken and grow. Instead of postponing spiritual development until we
have time to study systems unfamiliar to us, let's stay
alert to the spiritual work required of us each day.

*My spirit is awake throughout this day, as I stay caring
and connected with others and with myself.*

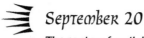

September 20

The poetry of earth is ceasing never

· · · · · · · · · · · · · ·

The poetry of earth is never dead.

JOHN KEATS

Everything that is alive changes. Over time, seeds become plants, fruits ripen, creatures are born and die. Over time, grief can turn to acceptance, pain can turn to joy. Change is inevitable in our lives. There are times when we can influence its direction by making choices that are more likely to result in positive, rather than negative, changes. Paths of spirituality and healing, like those of Twelve Step programs, change the effect that time's passage has on us. Committing ourselves to our values and visions, we open to the process of healing in ourselves and others. Time is on our side, as we develop a sense of our loving connection to others and of the usefulness of our example and service.

Today, I am unafraid of change. I meditate on an aspect of my life and notice whatever progress I have made over time.

September 21

Confession to another person, to a priest or a psychiatrist, is full of revelation. The self-understanding . . . brings cure and forgiveness! . . . Confession to divinity, to the essential life of what one loves and hopes, on a level other than the human, is full of revelation . . . has power to change one's life.

MURIEL RUKEYSER

Letting go of burdens, secrets, or shame is a way to cleanse the self. Traditional contexts for cleansing the self include religion and psychotherapy. Twelve Step programs offer additional opportunities to free ourselves of such burdens: sponsor-sponsee conversations, Step work, and sharing at meetings. Speaking with a trusted friend or keeping a journal also serves the process of letting go. Prayer, including writing letters to a Higher Power, can help us release guilt or anxiety. Writing letters to people living or dead, but not sending them, is a healing act, as is Tashlikh, the Jewish New Year custom of throwing bread that symbolizes misdeeds into a body of water that carries them away. If we wish, we can create our own rituals for letting go of spiritual burdens. Releasing secrets held within from fear or shame opens doors to healing, self-forgiveness, and new opportunity.

Today, I let go of mental and spiritual burdens.

September 22

I know they need me
I help to keep this whole show
Running

KATE RUSHIN

As lesbian, gay, bisexual, and transgender people, many of us began taking on adult responsibilities in childhood, if circumstances unfriendly to our difference taught us to be especially watchful and alert. Some of us learned overresponsibility from growing up in dysfunctional families that nurtured us inconsistently or inadequately. We may have developed rich imaginations—along with the habit of attempting to control people, places, and things around us.

Codependents assume responsibility for what others should do themselves. We consistently commit ourselves to more than we can handle, whether in work or play. We're burdened by perfectionism. We resent those for whom we sacrifice time and energy we'd prefer to use in other ways.

We can learn to be satisfied when we and others have done our best. Instead of stepping in to prevent others' discomfort, we must allow them to grow. We can let go of the need to have the answers. We can use the Al-Anon slogan "I didn't cause it, I can't control it, and I can't cure it."

Today, I feel the satisfaction of knowing
when I have done enough.

September 23

Within you there is a stillness and a sanctuary to which you can retreat at any time and be yourself.

HERMAN HESSE

Some of us associate meditation with occult practices that only specially trained people can engage in. But any of us can learn simple techniques that take us to the peace at the center of our being. Meditation can simply be sitting and observing the flow of breath as it enters and leaves our bodies. We may experience a sense of homecoming as we become one with our breathing, our bodies and minds relax, and struggle drops away from us.

It is no coincidence that the word *inspiration* literally means "breathing in." Sitting quietly and breathing naturally can refresh and energize our minds and bodies in only a few minutes. Seated in a relaxed position, spine straight, eyes closed or focused on a candle flame, we can simply inhale and exhale, letting go of all that is not of this moment. After a few minutes, we'll feel invigorated and calm, as if we've been to a special sanctuary or place of inspiration.

Today, meditation offers me a sanctuary.

September 24

Work should be performed in the spirit of worship.

NAPOLEON HILL

Whatever we have to do today, let's do it with complete attention and a whole heart. The moment will pass soon enough. Let's not lose the opportunity to live it fully, attentively, lovingly.

We can turn over whatever tasks we have to perform to the loving care of a Higher Power. We can pray for help. We can ask that the work we do may be of use to others and serve the purposes of our Higher Power. When we ask this and mean it, any resistance we may have to our work will be lifted. Whatever place we are in at this present moment, whatever work lies ahead, we have the opportunity to learn something. The more wholeheartedly we do our work, the more we are nourished by it.

Today, I love my work. I pray to be of use to my Higher Power as I do it.

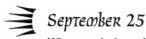

September 25

When an electron vibrates, the universe shakes.

SIR ARTHUR EDDINGTON

Some of us mistakenly believe that only the most vocal activists are important in our gay, lesbian, bisexual, and transgender communities or that only the most visibly successful creative artists among us matter in the world. We may feel small and insignificant, powerless to change conditions that we wish were different.

In truth, each one of us is a vital member of our communities and of the larger society, and each of us has a uniquely valuable contribution to make. All that we have experienced in the past, all that we are today, is of use to someone. When we share our experience, strength, and hope with others—whether one to one or at community gatherings, personal or spiritual growth groups, support groups, or Twelve Step meetings—we often are not aware of who is being reached by our stories and by our courage to speak. Each of our voices plays a role in the healing and growth of those around us.

Today, I am an essential part of my community and of the world.

Septembe 26

The eye through which I see God is the same eye through which God sees me; my eye and God's eye are one eye, one seeing, one knowing, one love.

MEISTER ECKHART

How often do we stop what we're doing to experience the unity of all things? Our daily lives often feel fragmented, rushed, weighed down with responsibilities. We may become so preoccupied by the problems and details of this day that we lose sight of the larger purposes of our lives.

Beyond the chaos and confusion of each day, we are part of something greater than ourselves. Our consciousness and our Higher Power's consciousness are one. We experience this unity when we enter into prayer and meditation. When we contemplate nature—and even sometimes when we're in the midst of a crowd of our fellow humans—we may be given glimpses of our connection with every other living being. Such moments of profound awareness come to us as a gift, reminding us that we are here to love ourselves, one another, and the Spirit that flows through all life.

Today, I see that my Higher Power unites me with all human beings.

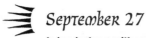 ## September 27

Lying is done with words, and also with silence.

ADRIENNE RICH

Most of us are fundamentally honest people who would not deliberately tell an untruth. But there are circumstances when we may fear to say all that we need to. In relationships, for example, we may allow confusion, discomfort, or resentment to build in ourselves or in a partner because of something we have left unsaid. We may assume that our feelings and wishes are known—or think that they somehow *ought* to be—when we haven't spoken them aloud.

Whatever the context of a particular relationship—romance, friendship, sponsorship, work— we must never assume that others can read our minds. They cannot, any more than we know what they want, need, or believe if they have not said so. We needn't assume that we will look bad if we reveal our ignorance; in fact, we sometimes must be willing to keep asking questions until we understand a situation.

Today, I have the courage to communicate my needs and wants and to ask questions of others.

September 28

*Yesterday is but a dream, tomorrow is but a vision.
But today well lived makes every yesterday a
dream of happiness and every tomorrow a vision
of hope. Look well, therefore, to this day.*

SANSKRIT PROVERB

Living in the present does not mean that we cannot
have goals or make plans. But obsessively regretting
the past or anticipating tomorrow's successes and
failures is like an anesthetic that keeps us from feeling whatever this moment holds. When fear or obsession keeps us from experiencing the present, we
lose its potential for pleasure as well as for pain. The
moment passes without our having experienced it.

It is often said by those recovering from addiction in Twelve Step programs that there are things
we can manage to do for one day that we couldn't
bear to contemplate doing for the rest of our lives.
We can follow this example and know that life is
whatever we are experiencing here and now, in this
day. It's not in our power to change the past or
know the future. What we have is the present. Let's
accept it as a gift.

Today, I keep my focus on the present.

 *September 29*

*Every grain of sap contains the full value
of the whole tree.*

MAHARISHI MAHESH YOGI

Have we made the right choices in our lives so far?
Should we be somewhere other than this place, job,
or relationship in which we find ourselves? When
we repeatedly ask such questions, we run the risk
of creating confusion and unhappiness.

We can make constructive changes when our
present situation is causing discomfort. If we look
within us for the source of our doubts, we can usually tell whether they come from a legitimate need
to change or if they are expressions of chronic self-
doubt, restlessness, and hopes of a "geographic
cure" for our problems.

Wherever we find ourselves today, there is a reason for our being here right now. We can find opportunities for learning, for connecting with our
fellow human beings, for giving service, for experiencing joy. No matter where we are in this world or
what we are doing, our Higher Power is with us.

Today, I bless the place I'm in.

September 30

To love oneself is the beginning of a life-long romance.

OSCAR WILDE

When Pride events, Twelve Step programs, therapists, and New Age gurus tell us that we have to learn to love ourselves, we may wonder if doing so will lead to self-absorption and selfishness. Shouldn't we be focusing on loving our fellow humans?

In truth, until we are capable of fully accepting and loving ourselves, the love we have to offer others is poor stuff indeed. Rejecting ourselves, even in small ways, clogs our communication with Spirit. Self-acceptance and unconditional love for our real selves are conditions of wholeness and spiritual health. When we have them, we are able to love others unselfishly, not needing to manipulate them to meet our needs, not clinging too tightly to them in fear of loneliness. When we are strong in our love and appreciation of ourselves, our spirits are large enough to care for others and to give freely, without hidden agendas. Self-love even helps us to serve our Higher Power with greater humility, gratitude, and courage.

Today, the love I offer myself without reservation increases love in the world around me.

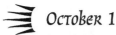

October 1

I need to be continually gathered back into the fold.

DAVID CRAWFORD

Step Ten suggests that we take a daily inventory of ourselves, continuing in the spirit of Step Four's searching and fearless review of our past.

We can take a few moments at any time during the day or evening for quiet reflection and review of the past twenty-four hours. We can list all that we're grateful for. Scanning our contacts with others, we can ask ourselves whether we've kept open the channels of truthful and caring communication. If there is something we wish we had done differently, rather than criticize or punish ourselves we can decide to remedy the situation at the earliest opportunity, admitting any mistakes and changing our behavior. If there are positive actions we've taken during the day—or actions we've wisely refrained from taking—we can acknowledge our progress. No inventory lists only deficits.

Let's also take a fresh look at our relationship with ourselves and ask whether we're treating ourselves with sensitivity and respect. Let's remember, too, to honor our relationship to Spirit and ask for help in cherishing the life force flowing through us.

Today, I review my actions in a spirit of gentleness and with faith in the possibility of progress.

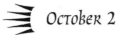# October 2

Solitude is one thing and loneliness is another.

MAY SARTON

At times, even the most independent among us feel lonely. Loneliness is a feeling that comes and goes in all human lives. It passes more easily when we simply acknowledge it without resisting or clinging to it. If we say to ourselves, not "I'm feeling my loneliness" but instead, "I'm feeling *the* loneliness," we are reminded of the universality of this feeling. Paradoxically, in doing so, we sense our connection to others. A sense of connection is one of the antidotes for loneliness.

Loneliness has little to do with being alone, physically apart from others. Who among us has never felt lonely in a room full of people? Solitude, on the other hand, can be accompanied by feelings of fullness, peace, and joy, when we use it as a medium for deep connection with ourselves and our Higher Power.

Today, I turn for comfort to the place deep within, where I know that I am connected with myself, others, and my Higher Power.

October 3

I want the hunger for love and beauty to be in the depths of my spirit, for I have seen those who are satisfied the most wretched of people. I have heard the sigh of those in yearning and longing, and it is sweeter than the sweetest melody.

KAHLIL GIBRAN

Physical hunger and thirst are valuable messages to ourselves from our bodies. Hunger and thirst remind us that we need the nourishment of food and of water in order to survive and flourish. Often, physical hungers are quite specific: we find ourselves craving particular foods containing minerals or other nutrients that need replenishing in the cells of our bodies.

Similarly, spiritual hunger and thirst are messages from our souls. We weren't created to live in isolation and deprivation. Our longing for love and our yearning for a sense of connection and purpose remind us that our spirits flourish when we feed our relationship to Spirit. Prayer, including asking our Higher Power for help and willingly offering help to others, fills us. Through our various hungers and their satisfaction, we come to know who we are and what our lives are meant for.

Today, I listen to my spirit's hunger and thirst. I feed my soul through prayer and service.

 OCTOBER 4

"How do you start to write a play, Mr. Williams?"
... "I start," he said sharply, "with a sentence."

GORE VIDAL
writing of playwright Tennessee Williams

Perhaps we cherish an ambition to accomplish something that, at this moment, seems beyond our means and talents. We aren't sure how to begin, yet the dream of accomplishment—some day far off—haunts us.

Few things come about instantly, and none magically. Most achievements are the result not of grandiosity but of processes that have had simple, straightforward beginnings. Patience and persistence, which bring dreams to fulfillment over time, involve many acts of beginning, as we recommit ourselves each day to continuing what we have started.

We can remove obstacles to long-range goals by seeing each task in simple terms. For example, if we wish to begin writing, we needn't think about becoming famous, making money, or gaining others' approval—all of which are beyond our control, in any case. Instead, we can plan to put words on paper. Writing begins with a sentence. Whatever it is we wish to accomplish, we can make a simple beginning.

Today, I begin at the beginning. I take a first step that brings me closer to fulfilling my desire.

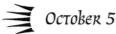

Octobeʀ 5

Homosexual survival lay in artifice, in plumage, in lampshades, sonnets, musical comedy, couture, syntax, religious ceremony, opera, lacquer, irony.

RICHARD RODRIGUEZ

Some of us dwell on how difficult life has been for us in the past. An unhappy childhood, a misunderstood adolescence, oppression by society at large—many gay, lesbian, bisexual, and transgender people have a sense of having survived past difficulties, both as individuals and as members of a community emerging from a history of discrimination.

We have not merely survived, but have flourished. While we know that stereotypes do not do justice to us in all our complexity, we think it no coincidence that gay, lesbian, bisexual, and transgender people are known for originality, creativity, humor, and style. We know, too, of the courage and commitment that our communities have shown in facing such continuing challenges as AIDS and prejudice.

As those recovering from addictions know, no matter how far downward we may have spiraled, recovery now makes it possible to put all of our past experiences to use in helping others to achieve sobriety. Let's acknowledge the unique gifts that have come to us as a result of overcoming past difficulties.

*Today, I am grateful for all of the days
that have led to this one.*

OctoBer 6

*He drank as a gut-punched boxer gasps for breath,
as a starving dog gobbles food—compulsively,
secretly, in pain and trembling. I use the past tense
not because he ever quit drinking but because he
quit living.*

SCOTT RUSSELL SANDERS

Some of us associate alcohol, drugs, and those who
use them with glamour and social grace. It is tempting to think that using is a sign of savoir faire, part
of a sophisticated lifestyle. Or perhaps we're attracted to others who suffer from addiction and believe we can help them overcome their problems.

While some may have choices where addictive
substances are concerned, many of us are driven by
compulsions that, if untreated, will progress. Addiction is a disease that has devastated many in gay,
lesbian, bisexual, and transgender communities.
Untreated, it leads to depression, spiritual isolation,
physical deterioration—even death. If we are using
or enabling others to use addictions, we must understand that willful control is not a sound substi-
tute for acceptance and recovery. There is nothing
glamorous about an addict's powerlessness. True
sophistication lies in knowing ourselves.

*Today, I do not glamorize what harms me. I look
honestly at my relationship to addictive substances
and behaviors.*

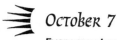

October 7

Every man has within himself the entire human condition.

MICHEL DE MONTAIGNE

It's tempting to compare ourselves with others and find ourselves wanting as a result. We see people who own more material things than we do, others who seem to have more friends or greater self-confidence than we have, and we judge ourselves to be somehow insufficient. Those who seem more gifted, advantaged, or successful than we are appear to "have it all." It doesn't occur to us that their inner experience doesn't necessarily match what we see on the surface. Others have hungers, griefs, fears, and insecurities much like our own. We may even have experience in areas of life that they haven't explored. We may have the capacity to help the same people we've thought of as better than ourselves. Instead of judging ourselves or others on the basis of external appearances, let's focus with appreciation on the spiritual journeys we share.

Today, I do not compare my insides with others' outsides.

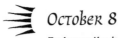 OCTOBER 8

Embrace the journey.

Saying heard in Twelve Step meetings

Our goals inspire us, and our plans help us take appropriate steps toward bringing our dreams and visions to fruition. But outcomes themselves are not the most important measure of our experience.

We cannot control outcomes. It is the process of our lives, the journey each of us takes, that is important. As we walk our paths today, we can experience our connection to the spirit within us, ask for help, encounter smooth or bumpy ground, appreciate the beauty we see. We can bring the devotion and energy of commitment to the day ahead of us. We have sufficient courage for this day. When we embrace the journey, each moment is an arrival in which we can feel joy.

Today, I relax and embrace the journey.

 *October 9*

The secret bores under the skin, gets in the blood, into the bone, and stays there.

SCOTT RUSSELL SANDERS

Certain things were never spoken of in our families or communities: deep, hidden anger; someone's unwanted behavior; perhaps our own sexuality. Pride, even survival, may have depended on keeping a secret. The price of consenting to keep a secret, then and now, is isolation. Although our attitudes may have changed toward events in the past, our old secrets live on in us in other forms, as shame, sickness, or anger.

We can break the cycle of old secrets. We don't have to preserve the patterns of a previous generation or of our own past. We release old secrets and the feelings that accompany them as we write them down or pray about them to our Higher Power. We can confide them to sponsors, counselors, or trusted friends. The secrets we feel most ashamed to speak are those most necessary to express. When we have safely let go of the burden of old secrets, of feelings of shame or rage, we feel immeasurably lighter and freer. Once a secret is told, it no longer has any power to harm us.

Today, healing begins with my willingness to speak.

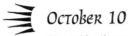 ## October 10

Blessed be the women who get you through.

ROBIN MORGAN

It is important to acknowledge those who support us in our lives. Even if we experience ourselves as independent, there are many who make our independence possible. Let's acknowledge those whose values and actions sustain us, those we meet in recovery whose sharing and example inspire us. Let's acknowledge those we trust to be supportive to us in difficulty, those with whom we share sorrows, and those with whom we share laughter. The people who care about us deserve our gratitude. They show us that we are not alone in the world.

We're sustained and strengthened not only by those with whom we have long and deep associations but also by those merely passing through our day. An act of courtesy, a look of kindness, a smile of recognition, a momentary sharing—these help form our sense of human interconnection and support.

Today, I am not alone. I am held and strengthened by a network of support.

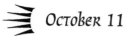 *October 11*

When a proud man hears another praised,
he thinks himself injured.

ENGLISH PROVERB

How do we react when a friend, co-worker, or member of our community receives recognition or rewards? Perhaps our impulse is one of warmth and gladness for his or her success. Or perhaps we focus on our own lack: we think how undeserving we are by comparison or believe that we are being unjustly overlooked. When we react to good fortune with self-rejection or envy, our hearts are seized with anger and bitterness.

We can respond to another's success with generosity, letting joy fill and expand us, when we recognize that each of us follows a special path. We don't have to compare our achievements with those of others in order to know that we are making progress. Our success is no less than anyone else's if we are true to ourselves, secure in doing what our spirit requires of us each day and understanding that we're works in progress. The universe contains an abundance of all that we need. By celebrating the ways we are richly blessed, we come to know that the experience of each one of us adds to the human family's wealth.

Today, another's success increases my own.

 OCTOBER 12

*All my life I've glorified sex, made it a drug
or a Queen.*

MARY ANN MCFADDEN

Is sex out of balance in our lives, occupying either
too much space or none at all? Some of us use sex
compulsively, as an anesthetic for undesired feelings.
Some are sexually "anorexic," fearing and avoiding
sexual expression. Perhaps we're reacting—whether
with excess or deprivation—to a society that prefers
that we keep our sexuality hidden or an upbringing
that taught us that our sexuality was wrong.

There may be times in our sexual history when
we haven't respected others or ourselves, when
we've been dishonest or irresponsible, letting fear
or shame shape our decisions. We can look searchingly at our feelings and behavior and acknowledge
what we would like to change in our relationship to
our sexuality. Our sexuality is one of the gifts of a
loving Higher Power. We can honor and celebrate
it as expression and as food for the soul, a way to
communicate love and caring for others and for
ourselves.

Today, I acknowledge and celebrate my sexual self.

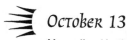 *October 13*

*I have lived in the present from time to time
and I can tell you that it is much overrated.*

PHILLIP LOPATE

Memory is one of our most valuable resources as
we affirm our acceptance of ourselves and our sense
of the rightness of where we are in our lives right
now. It reminds us that we have survived, evolved,
and flourished. It helps us affirm a hopeful vision of
the future. When we experience stress or fall into
discouragement, we can remember how far we have
come, how many mornings the sun has risen and
shone on us after fatigue and dejection the previous
night. We can accept momentary setbacks as simply
that, reminding ourselves that the larger picture is
one of progress.

A positive image or expectation energizes and
motivates us. When we let hope fill us, we can see
the truth and importance of a cherished dream and
let it inspire us to take appropriate actions today. We
needn't doubt that the universe will continue to take
care of us as we do our part, in the words of those in
Twelve Step recovery, by "showing up for life."

*Today, I have confidence in the process of my life.
I affirm the necessity of my past and trust in the
abundance of my future.*

October 14

Are we to look at cherry blossoms only in full bloom, the moon only when it is cloudless?

KENKO

What would happen if, for this day, we could remake our sense of beauty, naming each thing we see, each experience we encounter, as unique and valuable? We would refrain from judging ourselves, our circumstances, and others as insufficient or wrong. What we have seen as problems would become simply situations through which our Higher Power is guiding us. No weather would be bad weather, no face an ugly face, no event a defeat. We would find beauty in each person and each experience. Instead of hurrying to be elsewhere, we would cherish the present, aware of each moment as special and lovely.

We can begin to expand our sense of beauty by finding the good in something we formerly judged or simply ignored. Our world will look different to us if we see each thing as whole, exactly right as it is. Over time, its beauty will accumulate and transform our experience.

Today, I see unexpected beauty everywhere.
I am exactly where I'm supposed to be.

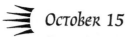 OctobeR 15

*Anger stirs and wakes in her; it opens its mouth,
and like a hot-mouthed puppy, laps up the
dredges of her shame.*
TONI MORRISON

We may have been taught that anger is wrong, that
maturity means learning to control it. Anger is a
natural and powerful feeling. We can choose not to
feed anger, perpetuate it, or let it become rage, but
we need not fear or suppress it. Clean, healthy
anger won't annihilate us or others. It can help us
to sense our limits. It can teach us what we feel passionate about. It can give us a new vision of ourselves, not as victims but as people with a sense of
justice and self-respect. If our voices have been un-
heard, our boundaries violated, or our identities
wrongly judged, anger can dissolve old, inhibiting
shame. Through it we can experience our strength
and clarity. We can permit others their anger, too,
by acknowledging that we hear them. We can experience the cleansing that anger initiates. Anger can
be a step toward healing.

*Today, I don't have to fear or fix emotions.
I acknowledge my feelings and those of others.*

October 16

I have met with but one or two persons in the course of my life who understood the art of Walking, that is, of taking walks,—who had a genius, so to speak, for sauntering.

HENRY DAVID THOREAU

In our rushed world, sauntering—literal or figurative—is often considered a fault. We wish that we or others would make faster progress, finish more speedily. Some of us jog as part of a fitness routine but rarely take a leisurely walk. We may feel that we don't have the time to enjoy the natural, easy movement of our bodies and the sights and sounds that surround us. Walking, while it gets us where we are going, can benefit us in numerous ways.

Walking gives us time to enjoy details along the way. There's no better way to get to know a new place. Walking can bring serenity by grounding us in the present moment. Many artists and thinkers find that walking before or after work inspires fresh solutions to problems. Some walk for health, some as a context for prayer or meditation. Walking, whether or not we have a destination in mind, is a chance to refresh ourselves with little expenditure of effort.

Today, I walk and breathe fresh air into my body and spirit.

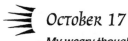 *October 17*

*My weary thoughts
play traitor to my soul.*

H. D.

The world we live in is to a great extent the world
our own thoughts create. It's easy to fall into negative habits of thought, perpetuating tired ideas and
attitudes without examining them. We may have
learned, and never questioned, patterns of negative
thinking from others. These thought patterns may
have taken a toll on us.

Our thoughts are powerful messages to ourselves. We can fetter our spirits with yesterday's
opinions and cultivate thoughts that weigh us down
with discouragement. Or we can entertain thoughts
that create energy, recharge our spirits, and change
our outlook.

Our souls love laughter and freedom. We can
choose to nourish our souls with attitudes and ideas
that produce joy and aliveness. The choice is ours.

*Today I let go of tired thoughts. I let a true sense of hope
nourish my soul on its journey.*

October 18

Grief is usually not a constant state, but instead often seems to occur in a series of waves of greater or lesser intensity.

DAVID HARP

When we're completely inundated with feelings of grief, we may be unable to see that we're in the midst of a process. We think that our sorrow cannot be healed, and that grief will never end. But just as we think we're about to go under, grief lessens for a moment. We forget ourselves, perhaps in giving service, offering compassion to another, or sharing laughter at a memory. This brief respite before grief returns hints at the healing that will come in time.

The moments between waves of grief are something like the moments of rest experienced between birth contractions by a woman in labor. Grief and healing, like many natural phenomena, are processes, not one-time events. Feelings of grief come and go, flooding us with intensity and then receding. Later, when the flow of grief has ended, a wave may still come over us now and then. Each of us has our own timetable; we can't predict when our grief will end. But we needn't fear that grief will destroy us or stay with us forever. In time, we do heal.

Today, I have compassion for myself and others who have suffered loss. I trust that healing will come eventually.

October 19

*A "whole person" is yet not whole. Each of us
seeks someone or some idea or God to complete
us. The phrase "whole person" does not mean an
individual who has need of nothing and no one.
Each of us needs more than herself, though we
do not all need or want the same thing.*

RITA LAPORTE

Our desires—especially our desires to be loved and
to be a part of something beyond ourselves—help to
teach us who we are and what our purpose is. Desire
reminds us of our need for others like ourselves.
It keeps us from forgetting that we are not alone.

From birth, each of us is connected with other
people, especially those in our communities and
chosen families. As we evolve, their experiences
inspire us to have faith in our own capacity for
healing, growth, and service. Through the spirit
within us, we're connected, too, to a Power greater
than ourselves. As we seek relationship with Spirit
and with people like ourselves, we can remember
the gifts we've been given, especially our ability to
give and receive love. The love we seek comes to us
as we give it. If what we desire is warmth, understanding, and connection, what we must do is offer
warmth, understanding, and connection to others.

*Today, I offer love to my Higher Power
through my love for others.*

October 20

Life was meant to be lived, and curiosity must be kept alive. One must never, for whatever reason, turn his back on life.

ELEANOR ROOSEVELT

The risk of suicide has sometimes been associated with gay, lesbian, bisexual, and transgender people. Unfortunately, the link persists, particularly among young people. Gay and lesbian teens are two to three times more likely than their heterosexual peers to commit suicide. To those with less freedom to express sexual nonconformity and without easy access to supportive communities, suicide may appear to be a way to escape isolation and low self-esteem.

We can have a healthy community only if we recognize the importance of making support and counseling available to everyone. We must refuse to consider suicide—including the slow suicide of addiction—as a rational option. If a friend threatens suicide, we can contact trained medical personnel.

If we ourselves feel driven to consider suicide, we must seek help. No matter how extreme our troubles appear, there is someone who will listen and help us begin the process of healing. We need not suffer alone or in silence. Now is the time for us to withstand any pull toward numbness or darkness and to embrace life.

Today, I choose life.

OctobeR 21

*Long after you have supposedly been cured of
malaria, the fever can flare up, the tremors can
shake you. So it is with the fevers of shame. . . .
The shame lingers in your marrow, and, because
of the shame, anger.*

SCOTT RUSSELL SANDERS

In certain situations, a wave of old shame unexpect-
edly rises up from the past and floods us. Why do
we feel shame? We may long ago have declared ourselves sexually liberated. We may be vocal in advo-
cating gay, lesbian, bisexual, and transgender rights.
We may be "out and proud." We thought we were
done with shame forever.

Releasing old feelings of shame and the anger
and frustration that accompany them is, like grieving, a gradual process. If we numbed ourselves with
addictive substances or compulsive behaviors during the coming-out process, we were emotionally
absent. We can acknowledge any ways we have
shut down in order to avoid hurt. Rather than deny
the shame, anger, or frustration we still carry, we
can place our spiritual baggage in the hands of people we trust and of a loving Higher Power. We can
move forward with true freedom.

Today, I release old shame. I am myself.

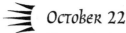 **October 22**

The art of being wise is the art of knowing what to overlook.

WILLIAM JAMES

We often receive good advice. Why, then, are we still imperfect? Why can't we do everything we've been told is good for us? Perhaps we're not ready to attempt perfection. Or perhaps we're not sure we ought to accept all the advice others offer. We may prefer to muddle through some of our difficulties in our own ways, letting experience and our inner guidance help us to discover what is true for us.

An expression often heard in Twelve Step meetings is "Take what you like and leave the rest." We can apply this principle of recovery to our lives, being selective about the advice we accept and the changes we undertake at any given time. Once we have committed ourselves to a new path, we can remember to be gentle with ourselves and not take on everything at once. There are appropriate moments for facing challenges. We can put tomorrow's demands on the shelf as we focus on our goals for today.

Today, I know my priorities.

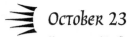 OCTOBER 23

I'm so used to fighting with you
I don't know how not to.

EDWARD FIELD

For some of us, fighting—physically or verbally—
is a reflex. We may take almost instant exception
to what a lover, friend, or co-worker says. We
may even be our own adversaries, objecting to our
thoughts or feelings the moment we've felt or expressed them. We may not know how to stop seeing
antagonists wherever we look.

　　The inner strength that comes from self-acceptance
allows us to live comfortably in a world where there
are many conflicting opinions. When we are confident that we know how to express our wants and
needs, we're less likely to see others as invasive or
hostile. Our knowledge of our boundaries gives us
poise and patience—even a sense of humor. Secure
in our self-knowledge and self-love, we can let go
of our habit of resisting everything. A wide array of
possible responses then becomes available to us.

Today, I respond, rather than reacting with argument.

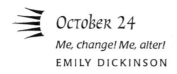

October 24

Me, change! Me, alter!

EMILY DICKINSON

Perhaps experiencing ourselves as gay, lesbian, bisexual, or transgender in a world that opposes our unconventional sexual identity has required us to declare assertively who we are. Once we've come out, our communities may seem closed to complexity or further change.

Often, however, making a strong declaration brings up its opposite; as soon as we've said we'll never again experience a particular desire, that is the very desire we feel. Whether or not we act on it, we may feel momentarily confused. We needn't assume we were wrong to come out or feel that we have betrayed our principles by entertaining a "politically incorrect" feeling. In time, more will be revealed. We can trust time and our own deep feelings—far better than trends or the needs of others—to reveal the complex nature of our true identity.

*Today, I embrace the complexity
of my feelings and identity.*

October 25

And so at last I climbed
the honey tree, ate
chunks of pure light.

MARY OLIVER

When we let go of the self-destructive behavior of addiction or a constricting conformity, we begin to know what joy is. We experience the freedom of knowing and being ourselves. Our energy is no longer being used to hold on to old, limiting systems of thought or action. Our spirits are freed. We are awake and alive.

Joy is not an emotion reserved for a privileged few. All of us have the capacity to feel joy. Joy does not depend on things and circumstances outside ourselves but on our willingness to receive it. We feel joy when we remove the obstacles to communication with our own spirit and to our relationship with a Higher Power. Once we begin to feel joy, it becomes clear how natural a state it is. Joy is not only possible, but necessary. Our souls require it.

Today, I let joy flow through me.

October 26

It is easy, terribly easy, to shake a man's faith in himself. To take advantage of that to break a man's spirit, is devil's work.

GEORGE BERNARD SHAW

How tempting to think that something makes us superior to others. How thoughtlessly we reveal this attitude in our words or manner. All of us are connected at the root. If we show contempt for any other person, we are showing contempt for ourselves.

As gay, lesbian, bisexual, and transgender people, we know how vulnerable we have been to others' attitudes toward us. We know something about the damage that is caused by intolerance and the healing that is brought about by true respect. Let's not forget the lessons of the past. Let's take care not to set ourselves up as judges or presume to punish others. By practicing genuine respect and care for others, we ultimately strengthen our self-respect.

Today, I set my ego aside. I harm no one.

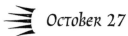 ## October 27

Legends are fine if you've got somebody who loves you, some man who's not afraid to be in love with Judy Garland.

JUDY GARLAND

Fame is sometimes a matter of talent and sometimes a matter of luck; in either case, it is not something within our control. Nonetheless, fame—our own or others'—often plays a part in our fantasies. Many gay, lesbian, bisexual, and transgender people crave the spotlight, and some of us manage to achieve some kind of fame within our own communities or in the wider world. Those who have it know first-hand that instead of solving human problems, fame simply gives rise to a different variety of them.

Whatever our degree of success or visibility, we all face the challenge of finding satisfaction in our lives and work. Fulfillment cannot be conferred from the outside. When we respect the needs of the spirit that moves within us, when we accept our limitations and do the best we can with our gifts, when we understand what we can and cannot control, we will take fame or the lack of it in stride. We will not confuse appearances with life.

Today, I recognize the difference between image and reality. I know myself and am content.

October 28

*I love a gay and sociable wisdom, and shun
harshness and austerity in behavior, holding
every surly countenance suspect.*

MICHEL DE MONTAIGNE

Some of us equate right living with humorlessness
and sacrifice. We avoid adult responsibilities, imagining that they will imprison us. We shun people in
recovery, fearing that they will try to convert us to
a life without pleasure.

The opposite is true. Becoming accountable to
ourselves and others releases the powerful energy
and laughter of those who have faced the destruction within themselves. Responsibility makes possible a path of personal fulfillment that exposes the
deprivation and restriction of living only for oneself.
Assuming adult responsibilities—not the same as
playing the role of martyr or of cultivating resentments—helps us to name and know ourselves and to
connect through service with other members of the
human family. It feeds our hunger to be of use.

*Today, the laughter of a light spirit
connects me with others.*

October 29

*For the eye has this strange property: it rests
only on beauty; like a butterfly it seeks colour
and basks in warmth.*

VIRGINIA WOOLF

The world is full of beauty that speaks through our
senses directly to our souls. It seems that we were
made for beauty; something within us seeks it, de-
lights in it, and recognizes it as nourishment and
truth. Beauty is not hard to find; we encounter it
everywhere in our day.

Beauty comes to us at unexpected moments, as
a gift, and we can also seek beauty intentionally. In
the midst of a hectic schedule, whether we live in
the city or country, we can stop what we're doing
for a few minutes and listen to a piece of music,
read a poem, or take a short walk that gives us a
view of sky, earth, water, or growing things. A
glimpse of beauty changes our outlook more effectively than drinking coffee or alcohol. It is surprising how little it takes to refresh our spirits. A brief
change of scene or focus, the warmth of human
contact, or a few moments of breathing in the
peace of Spirit give us rest and renewed energy.

Today, I seek beauty and find it everywhere.

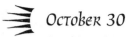 *October 30*

*A real book is not one that we read,
but one that reads us.*

W. H. AUDEN

The books that are most memorable and useful,
those to which we return again and again, are the
ones in which our own souls are somehow mirrored
and illuminated. These are not as rare as one might
think. A collection of poems or essays that exam-
ines reality in depth, a novel that tells a story that
reminds us of our own struggles, a spiritual work
that responds to our yearning for connection with
self and Spirit—any of these, and still others, can
help us on our journey.

    We turn to books to inform, motivate, and en-
courage us. Reading helps satisfy our hunger to
understand other people's lives and visions as we
shape a vision of our own. Through reading, we
can connect deeply with ourselves. Let's seek out
books that truly "read us."

*Today, I read something that offers me a focus
for my day and light for my spirit.*

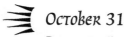 OCTOBER 31

*Does my mother know? Hmmm. My mother
knows, but she doesn't know.*

GINA TAYLOR

Perhaps growing up with an awareness of our difference from others, we were especially conscious
of the giving and withholding of approval by family
and institutions. Though we may have experienced
some understanding and tolerance, we're not likely
to have received society's approval as lesbians, gay
men, bisexuals, or transgender people. As is often
the case when something has been withheld from
us, many of us have focused on approval and have
craved it.

An inordinate desire for approval leads to aban-
doning our real selves and focusing on what we
imagine to be the needs and desires of others. Seeking approval, effacing ourselves, becomes a habit in
human relationships—even those in which approval
is offered to our authentic selves. Underneath our
craving for approval, it is love that we desire.
Approval is not love and will never lead to love.

Love has no conditions. It takes us as we are.
Giving it and receiving it satisfies our soul's hunger
as no exchange of mere approval ever will.

Today, I love and am loved.

November 1

Sought through prayer and meditation to improve our conscious contact with God as we understood Him, . . .

Step Eleven of the
Twelve Steps of Alcoholics Anonymous

Step Eleven's reference to conscious contact suggests that prayer is a means of sustaining a relationship with a Power greater than ourselves. By emphasizing the words "as we understood Him," this Step leaves the concept of a Higher Power up to us. We needn't be limited by the pronoun "Him." Our sense of a Higher Power may be a traditional one or may include any of the ways we experience our spirits in relationship with a larger Spirit—a presence beyond our own egos.

Whatever our religious beliefs—or the absence of them—we can have a spiritual practice that raises our awareness. In addition to traditional forms of prayer or meditation, we can reflect on our actions, study spiritual literature, and cultivate gratitude through making lists of all that we appreciate. We can seek to become more aware of how our thoughts, words, and actions reverberate through our lives and communities, how they ripple outward and affect the wider world.

Today, I further my relationship with my Higher Power by raising my awareness of the effects of what I think, say, and do.

 November 2

*... praying only for knowledge of His will for us
and the power to carry that out.*

Step Eleven of the
Twelve Steps of Alcoholics Anonymous

Lesbian, gay, bisexual, and transgender people may
have had negative experiences with various forms
of authority. We may question Step Eleven's urging
that we seek to know a Higher Power's will. We
may suspect that doing so is a way to negate our
identities and desires.

We needn't think of our Higher Power's will
for us as conflicting with our own. The spirit within us is a part of the Spirit to whom we speak in
prayer. In our heart of hearts, we know the purpose
for which we've been given this life to live. At times
we may have been sidetracked—by fear, rebellious-
ness, shame, or self-rejection—but we have always
wanted to carry out this purpose.

Higher awareness requires that we become conscious of and connected with ourselves. Prayer and
meditation are among the means of communication
we may use to deepen this connection. As we grow
in self-acceptance and become more intimate with
our true selves, we discover our purpose and the way
to fulfill it.

*Today, I listen to my heart of hearts.
I align my life with the desires of my spirit.*

November 3

It is . . . necessary to be suspicious of those who seek to convince us with means other than reason, and of charismatic leaders: we must be cautious about delegating to others our judgment and our will. Since it is difficult to distinguish true prophets from false, it is as well to regard all prophets with suspicion.

PRIMO LEVI

Learning to trust our own judgment may be one of our greatest challenges. In the process of claiming our gay, lesbian, bisexual, and transgender identities, we've had some experience of listening to our inner guidance even when it conflicted with what others told us. We may not always be confident, however, especially in the seductive presence of charismatic people. Within our own communities, as in the wider world, there are strong, persuasive voices claiming to have a monopoly on the truth.

Who are we? What do we value? What must we do? These are spiritual questions; the answers are profoundly personal. When a candid friend or counselor mirrors our true selves back to us, we see more clearly what we've already sensed about ourselves, and we are able to make independent decisions. Decisions that proceed from self-knowledge and self-trust are decisions worthy of us.

Today, I trust my knowledge of who I am.

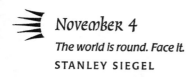

November 4

The world is round. Face it.

STANLEY SIEGEL

Gay, lesbian, bisexual, and transgender—we who name ourselves in these ways are part of a vast and varied humanity. We are among the essential ingredients in the recipe for the human race. Whether others are comfortable or uncomfortable with our presence, they must live side by side with us on this planet. We, too, must live here with others who are different from us. Recognizing that we—and they—belong here equally is the first step toward mutual respect and peace.

When we cry out for recognition and tolerance from others, let's remember that we must first be willing to offer recognition and tolerance to ourselves. Self-love and self-acceptance are more powerful than any rejection. We must be willing, too, to love and accept those who are not of our community. Our embrace of variety and difference has an impact on the evolving consciousness of those who inhabit our round planet along with us.

Today, I include and embrace all members of the human family.

November 5

Father's drinking became the family secret.

SCOTT RUSSELL SANDERS

Few families in this country have been entirely spared the impact of addiction to drugs or behaviors. Fortunately, we're living in a time when the secrets of family addictions are finally being spoken aloud and shared. With sharing, the devastation of secrecy has been diminished, and the doors to healing are open.

If we grew up in a family in which someone suffered from addiction we may have become over-responsible, controlling, secretive, or emotionally shut down. Addiction in the family, even generations back, has powerful, continuing effects, until someone is able to stop the pattern.

Addiction is a disease, not a moral failure. Treatment through Twelve Step programs is a powerful way to break the cycle of addiction. Sharing the language of recovery, we're no longer required to walk through life alone, bearing the burden of a family secret.

*Today, I share my story with others
and let healing enter.*

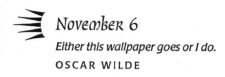

November 6

Either this wallpaper goes or I do.

OSCAR WILDE

Each day of our lives, there are choices to make in both large and small things. Most of us face the larger decisions—the work we do, the friends with whom we associate, where we call home—actively and consciously. But every choice we make expresses our spirits and shapes our lives.

Questions arise throughout each day: will we go to a meeting, be aware of how we spend money, choose healthful foods, or reach out to another person with warmth and kindness without waiting for him or her to do so first? We often take actions automatically, only dimly aware that each choice has far-reaching consequences. We choose to live each day feeling either grumpy and resentful or grateful and open. Passivity—believing that things simply happen to us—is also a choice. Making choices is an expression of the life spirit that flows through us. We can choose thoughts and attitudes that help create a day of beauty, energy, and love.

Today, I make conscious choices.

 ## November 7

*By the time I found my voice to speak,
Jacqueline was gone.*

LESLIE FEINBERG
Stone Butch Blues

Finding our authentic voices and using them with courage has been crucial to our survival as gay, lesbian, bisexual, and transgender people. Act Up's slogan "Silence = Death" expresses it succinctly. The slogan reminds us that speaking out, rather than accepting the status quo as unchangeable, can be a life-or-death matter.

There are also times when having the wisdom and forbearance to keep silent is an appropriate and powerful choice. When our words would be premature, cause serious harm, or intensify a conflict to no purpose, we keep silent.

We have opportunities each day to speak or be silent. For some of us, speaking up is a challenge, especially if we fear that our words may cause inconvenience, discomfort, or anger. For others, the choice to keep silent, giving ourselves or others time to assimilate a thought or feeling, is a genuine challenge. If we speak carelessly or keep silence too long, we may perpetuate a habit that defines our approach to life. As we go through our day, we can let go of our fear of words or of stillness, honoring the truth by speaking up or keeping silent.

Today, I know when to speak and when to keep silent.

November 8

Paradoxically, the source of the question is the answer it seeks. "What would I be without God?"
Consider this question from your inner awareness. Not you the noun, the person you may think you are, but you the verb, the process of being in full relationship, continuously, with its creator.

DAVID A. COOPER

Rather than debate whether a Higher Power exists, we can live in conversation with Spirit. We aren't required to perpetuate the notion of God as a dictatorial parent and of us as obedient or rebellious children. Remembering that we ourselves aren't God, we can be mindful of our role as cocreators of the world we inhabit. We have an active role in our response to the mystery of life—in the attitudes and behavior we cultivate.

We can turn from debating what we know or don't know and take a few moments to close our eyes and experience awe. Mystery is an aspect of all we encounter: the unfolding of the natural world, the abundance and variety of people, the complexity of our thoughts, the immensity of the universe. We can merge with this sense of awe and retain it throughout the day, experiencing each moment as the center of creation.

Today, I experience awe.

November 9

In the middle of the journey of our life
I came to my senses in a dark forest,
for I had lost the straight path.

DANTE
Inferno, translated by H. R. Huse

The phrase "midlife crisis" identifies a time when many people feel a critical need to reevaluate their direction and choices. This need isn't limited to midlife: there are times throughout life when we feel lost or confused. We wonder whether we're wasting our time, yet we doubt that we know how to make changes and question whether the changes we're considering are necessary and right.

Doubt and confusion are a wake-up call to our spirits. Something in us thirsts for clear vision and purpose, for the renewal of motivation and energy that comes with knowing who we are and where we intend to go. Now is a time for faith and willingness, for trust that a Higher Power will bring us clarity. The answers to our questions are already present. We may experience them as sudden inspiration, or we may discover them gradually through attending meetings, support groups, or classes. We may quietly go within, using prayer or meditation. When we remain open to new understanding, it comes.

Today, I trust that there is a clearing in the woods.

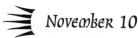 *November 10*

They are like trees planted near flowing rivers,
which bear fruit when they are ready.
Their leaves will not fall or wither.
Everything they do will succeed.

PSALM 1:3
translated by Stephen Mitchell

When we aren't ready to recognize a truth, accept
a need to make changes, or bring new attitudes to
old situations in our lives, our efforts and exertions
may seem to go nowhere. The moment we are entirely ready, things begin to flow easily. We do with
ease and pleasure what we formerly found difficult.
We wonder what all our struggling was about.

   We needn't see challenges as arduous. Instead,
we can remind ourselves of everything we have
going for us. We can remember past experiences
that have helped prepare us for this one. We can
look at our gifts and our willingness to learn and
grow. We're not alone, and we can ask for help.
Our Higher Power does not give us more than we
can handle.

I have the resources within me to handle the challenges
and joys this day brings.

November 11

I now look at the past with love and choose to learn from my old experiences. . . . The past is over and done.

LOUISE HAY

Among the obstacles to our serenity may be recurrent regrets about past actions and events, not only those choices that were within our control but also circumstances and occurrences over which we were powerless. Focusing on a sense of victimization or self-blame concerning the past is a block to growth and to the fulfillment of our spirit's longings.

If we have unfinished business—amends or restitution that we owe and that are within our power to carry out—we must take appropriate actions. But once we've cleaned house, we must no longer dwell painfully in the past. We can look back with compassion at ourselves and others from a mature, loving perspective. We can treasure past mistakes and sorrows as our teachers. We can be whole, healed, fully present, and fully loving.

Today, I have grown beyond my past.
I look at it lovingly and let it go.

November 12

Whatever the world thought was wrong with me
I finally began to agree was right.
LESLIE FEINBERG

As lesbian, gay, bisexual, and transgender people,
we've developed a sensitive awareness of others'
reactions, overt or subtle, to our sexuality or gender
identity. Negative images may have entered our consciousness from an early age, before we found affirmation and support for our nonconformity, perhaps
before we fully understood who we were. Have we
let our self-images be shaped by how others see us?
We must recognize and address old habits of self-
rejection in order to let go of them. When we list our
qualities, which words and phrases come to mind?
We can note any negative terms and ask ourselves
how they became part of our self-portrait. We can
ask our Higher Power for help in removing negative
self-images. We can visualize positive images entering us with each intake of breath, negative thoughts
leaving us with each exhalation. We can affirm that
there is no room in our lives for self-rejection.

Today, I let go of old, negative judgments of myself
and become willing to receive positive images. I see
myself as whole and lovable.

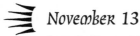 *November 13*

*I am choking on words
that have gone down the wrong way.*
IMANI HENRY

When someone's words or behavior toward us hurts, we may react automatically. Some of us shoot back words intended to convey anger or scorn. Some of us swallow our reaction and let it ferment inside us, perhaps mixing shame with resentment. Both of these reactions perpetuate hurt, but we have other options.

We can say honestly to the person whose action has affected us, "That hurts!" By keeping it simple, by not blaming, we can simply acknowledge our reaction. We can separate our reaction from the trigger and let go of the hurt we experience.

We must remember our own maturity and generosity. We know that beneath the hostility of others is fear or self-doubt, and that beneath their anger is a capacity for love and kindness.

*Today, I let go of hurt and cultivate love
and understanding.*

 November 14

*For what shall it profit a man, if he shall gain
the whole world, and lose his own soul?*

MARK 8:36

Some of us have ambitious visions of what we're
supposed to achieve. We're working to fulfill long-
cherished desires for success, however we've defined it. Perhaps we're trying to make up for time
"lost" while we redefined our sexual or gender
identity or healed from illness or addiction. Desire
for approval from family and peers may motivate
us to work especially hard at what we do.

Spiritual practice may be on our list of things to
do later, after we've achieved our goals. But there is
no later. We have this day, this moment. The selves
we're hoping to become in the future must be part
of our process of getting there. Time to relax, laugh,
breathe, and cultivate communication with a Higher
Power is well used. Taking a brief period each day to
sit in stillness and greet the spirit within us, we become attuned to our own deep wisdom, needs, and
rhythms. Whatever else we have on the agenda can
then flow with greater ease.

Today, I let my spirit breathe.

November 15

I was sick to death of ambiguities, and only wished to be known for what I was and dwell with her in the palace of truth.

LADY UNA TROUBRIDGE
longtime companion of Radclyffe Hall

Is there something about us that we know to be true and yet have not acknowledged to ourselves or to others we trust?

We are entitled to privacy; we are not required to express every thought or feeling at all times and places. But we may sometimes keep silent from fear of appearing ridiculous or from a belief that we are insufficient or unworthy people. Perhaps we have fostered an atmosphere of ambiguity as a way of protecting ourselves from others' opinions or reactions. Acknowledging what is true for us clears the air, frees us from the burden of concealment, and brings us into more genuine relationships with others. Our courage in acknowledging the truth can help deepen intimacy. It helps create an atmosphere in which others, too, are freer to be open and genuine. Whether in our communities or in one-to-one connections, we bring light and freedom when we have the willingness to be known for who we are.

Today, I have the courage and integrity to be myself with others.

November 16

I have loved, and I have been loved,
and all the rest is just background music.

ESTELLE RAMEY

What we accomplish, own, or collect is less important than having people in our lives for whom we
really care and who really care for us. They are the
people who are close to us and with whom we can
share ourselves. They are the people with whom we
can be vulnerable. They help when we are sick or in
trouble. They nourish our self-esteem and the life
force flowing through us. They are lovers, friends,
members of our biological families or our families
of choice. We have loving relationships, too, with
our Higher Power, with animals, and with members
of the extended communities and support networks
that give us feelings of familiarity and safety.

Loving feelings not only enhance life and health;
they are necessary. We need never complain that we
lack love; the love we impart to others is as valuable
and healing as love we receive. If we want more love
in our lives, all we need do is give it.

Today, I am healed by giving and receiving love.

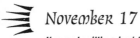 ## November 17

*I'm not willing just to be tolerated. That wounds
my love of love and of liberty.*

JEAN COCTEAU

As we continue to grow, we may recognize that
there are people in our lives whose values and attitudes no longer fit with our own. When we do perceive that a particular association has ended, we can
detach from it lovingly, without harming others or
ourselves. We are simply acknowledging the truth
of change.

We can continue to nurture long-standing relationships with friends who have shared our journey
and who offer warmth and support. We can reach
out to new people we admire, whose outlook and
convictions resonate with our own; some will respond as potential friends.

When we choose the company of others who
are on our mental, moral, and spiritual wavelength,
we are affirmed in our identities and inspired to
seek deeper levels of awareness. The intelligent
laughter of our peers' responses to life stimulates
our aliveness.

*Today, my relationships are evolving. I enjoy the
company of those who are on my wavelength.*

November 18

And may the blessed name of holiness be hailed, though it be higher than all the blessings, songs, praises, and consolations that we utter in this world.

THE MOURNERS' KADDISH

Kaddish, an ancient Aramaic prayer traditionally recited in synagogues by those in mourning for friends or loved ones, makes no mention of death or loss. Instead, those who speak it are affirming that our world is filled with holiness beyond anything we can imagine or name in our prayers.

Our sense of holiness comes to us in large part through the love that we feel for other people and the ways that our lives are touched by theirs. Our love and caring for one another teaches us what we know about the great, unimaginable love that is Spirit.

Love is more powerful than physical loss or the passage of time. Death does not change love. Though we mourn those who are no longer with us, their gifts remain and continue to transform us. We experience holiness in the ways their lives have touched our own. In time, we sense that those who have blessed us with their presence are teaching us with the example of their lives.

Today, I rejoice in the love that has touched my life.

November 19

Total absence of humor renders life impossible.

COLETTE

How do we keep things in their proper perspective, neither denying the importance of problems we must address nor giving equal weight and attention to everything that concerns us?

Talking with those we trust and reasoning things through together can help us to establish our priorities. Attending a Twelve Step meeting, counseling session, or spiritual service; sitting in meditation; or simply taking a walk and breathing fresh air can help lift unnecessary burdens from our spirits.

One of the most effective ways to cope with a difficult situation is to lighten our hearts with humor. We can laugh or smile—gently, never unkindly—at ourselves and the challenges we face. We can see that our problems are simply situations. We remember that we're "works in progress"—humans among humans with similar imperfections and challenges.

Today, my sense of humor helps me keep a balanced outlook.

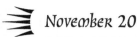 *November 20*

*But they delight in the way things are
and keep their hearts open, day and night.*

PSALM 1:2
translated by Stephen Mitchell

Many things are going right in our lives today. We
need not focus our attention and energies on the
one or two things we may be experiencing as wrong.
Instead, we can choose to remember and praise each
of the things for which we are grateful.

We can praise life itself and our chance to live it
and enjoy it in this unique moment. We can praise
the beauty of nature, people, and animals, and
count the gifts our world offers to each of our five
senses. We can be glad of our many chances to be
of service to others. As lesbian, gay, bisexual, and
transgender people, we can praise the opportunities
we've been given to express nonconforming sexual
or gender identities. We can affirm and celebrate
our friends and networks of support. Each thing
we focus our attention on is transformed in our
consciousness by our act of praising.

Today, I am a singer of praise.

November 21

I've never outraged Nature. I've always listened to her advice and followed it wherever it went.

JOE ORTON

Nature, so often referred to as our Mother, is brimming over with diverse creative impulses. She expresses herself in a seemingly endless variety of ways. We, like the natural world, are blessed with intelligent impulses that lead us on our journeys.

Instead of doubting ourselves, we can give ourselves credit for the innate wisdom nature has given to us. Our bodies tell us when they need rest, food, movement, touch, and healing tears. Similarly, what we call intuition or inner guidance lets us know what will meet our mental and spiritual needs, where the solutions to our problems lie, and what the next step ought to be in our process of becoming our true selves. Instead of being sidetracked or confused by others' expectations or judgments, we can go within and listen to our deep dreams and desires.

Today, as I make decisions, I honor my innate wisdom.

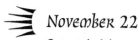# November 22

Success is doing exactly as one pleases.

ISAAC MIZRAHI

We've been taught since childhood that it's wrong to be selfish. We don't want to see ourselves as selfish or be seen that way by others. But there is a kind of selfishness that is healthy and that ultimately benefits others.

When those in Twelve Step recovery repeat the slogans "Keep the focus on yourself" and "This is a selfish program," they're alluding to principles that can be useful to all of us. We may choose to be "selfish" when we honor our commitments in the face of stress, peer pressure, or conflicting demands. Honoring our beliefs—no matter what—strengthens our sense of self. When the survival and health of our spirits means speaking the truth of our gay, lesbian, bisexual, or transgender identities, we must be willing to upset the status quo in our families or communities. To be "selfish" in the best sense of the word is to be true to ourselves and our vision.

Today, I recognize the importance of my beliefs, and I honor them as a valuable part of myself.

November 23

I started taking the pills last February. By March my "viral load" tested undetectable.... It took awhile to come to terms with the good news, somehow.

NEIL GREENBERG

Good news can be as challenging, in its own way, as bad. We may be resistant and find it hard to trust at first. It may upset long-held expectations and require changes in the way we see ourselves and our possibilities. It may require that we let go of a familiar image of ourselves and of our lives as we face the uncertainties of the future.

We can keep hope alive by being prepared to receive good news. Our willingness to receive it can invite it to manifest in our lives. Whether or not the news we receive is what we call good, we continue to be worthy and good people. We must not derive our sense of ourselves and our possibilities from the news we receive, even the so-called good news. But we must stay open to recognizing the truth of good news when we hear it.

Today, I welcome truth; it is always good news.

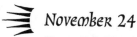 *November 24*

Live as if you liked yourself, and it may happen.....
Every gardener knows that after the digging, after
the planting, after the long season of tending and
growth, the harvest comes.

MARGE PIERCY

Patience comes not only from faith that we will
succeed at some time far in the future, but also
from cultivating the habit of staying in the present,
calmly doing what each day requires. Patience can
be a spiritual practice, as we rest in the serenity that
all is well and that we are exactly where we should
be at this moment.

Affirming that all is well with ourselves and our
world is neither denial nor passivity; it is an ener-
getic statement of faith that the actions we are taking toward healing, repair, and growth are good in
themselves, whatever their outcomes. We can be
poised and calm as we live each day in appreciation
of ourselves, our many gifts, and our opportunities
for service.

Today, I have the composure that comes from knowing I
am where I should be. My patience brings peace of mind.

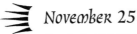 *November 25*

Beauty is a mystery. You can neither eat it nor make flannel out of it.

D. H. LAWRENCE

What would happen if we took time out today for something seemingly impractical, something that had nothing at all to do with finishing tasks, earning a living, improving health, or even helping others? Visiting a garden or an architecturally interesting building, listening to music for its own sake rather than as the background for some other activity, beginning to read a work of literature we thought we had no time for, creating something artistic for the pleasure of it rather than for others' approval—these are a few examples of the infinite number of ways we can come into the presence of beauty.

Beauty is a doorway to ourselves. It may bring us to an inner self that is filled with creative impulses or to a still and peaceful inner sanctuary where we sense our union with others and with Spirit. Beauty and our response to it make us feel more human—and more nearly divine.

Today, I include beauty in my life, not as something useful but for its own sake.

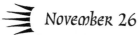

November 26

It was a little scary to be that self-disclosing. After all, like most people, I usually want to show my best side, not my darkest moments.

DEAN ORNISH

Some of us have experienced moments of despair in the recent or distant past. Whether we experienced loss or failure or were successful in the eyes of others, our spirits seemed to hit bottom. We may have faced the darkness of isolation, depression, addiction, violence, or even thoughts of suicide—whatever, for us, was extreme darkness. When we acknowledged the depth of our trouble and our sense of powerlessness over it, our souls responded and our lives began to turn around.

Our experience of hopelessness has given us strength and a greater love of each day. It is for this very reason that sharing our past with friends, family, and community members is a gift. We know firsthand that it's possible to begin again and to embrace life, no matter what bleakness we once faced. Sharing our experience, strength, and hope not only helps others emerge from their own darkness, but gives them permission to speak the truth about their journeys and continue the process of healing.

Today, I offer my journey as an example.

November 27

*The Zen monk didn't talk about man's
shortcomings, our undeservedness, or the
necessity of suffering. He talked about being
happy. He talked about how if we were happy
and kind, we would pass this happiness and
kindness on to the people around us, and they
would be happier and kinder, too.*

DINTY W. MOORE

In thinking of what lies ahead of us each day, we
may focus on whether or not we're adequate to the
problems we'll be called upon to face. We may let
anxiety or critical judgment shape our vision of
ourselves, or believe that what's required of us is
sacrifice and endurance. We can take a different
approach to the day and to our role in it.

Instead of looking for defects in the day or in
ourselves, we can affirm that all is deeply right with
us and with what we experience. We can take pleasure in the familiar and remain open to the new,
keeping the accent on gratitude and lightness. We
can smile at friends and strangers and take in the
warmth of returned smiles. We can keep our hearts
light by seeking ways to be kind to others.

*Today, I cultivate a light heart. I let my kindness and
happiness shine.*

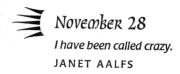

November 28

I have been called crazy.

JANET AALFS

In affirming our lesbian, gay, bisexual, or transgender identities and other expressions of our originality, we've overturned assumptions and expectations of society, teachers, families, and peers—in many cases, even of ourselves. One strategy others may use to dismiss anything that disturbs their vision of an orderly universe is to call it crazy. We, too, may have leveled the charge of mental illness at ourselves—a cruel but effective way to avoid the truth of our nonconformity.

Real mental illness is a serious problem, not to be lightly dismissed when it really exists. It causes great suffering and sometimes death; it requires expert treatment. It should not be confused with the moments of confusion, self-doubt, or avoidance to which any of us may be subject.

Let's affirm our sanity, which is another term for health and wholeness. If we hold ourselves in high esteem and proclaim and cherish our originality, we can bring light and healing to others.

Today, I replace self-doubt with affirmations of mental and spiritual health.

November 29

*It is time we start applauding each others'
freedom, choices, and movement—
in many different directions.*

JUANA MARIA GONZALEZ PAZ

Do we take the gifts bestowed on us by others'
daring, originality, and accomplishment for granted?
Or worse, are we uncomfortable with controversy
and difference and wish our peers would fade into
the woodwork once in a while?

The members of our gay, lesbian, bisexual, and
transgender families and the community of those in
Twelve Step recovery are true originals, making
new maps of possibilities. Their courage is creating
new paths of experience that broaden our options
and inspire us to honor our own inner truths. We all
need one another's appreciation and support to give
us courage to continue. Instead of rejecting difference or taking it for granted, we can consciously
support it. Speaking a few words or writing a note
of acknowledgment and thanks is a seemingly small
gesture, but it goes from our heart to another's. Our
generosity creates and sustains our freedom.

*Today, I express heartfelt appreciation for the freedom
and variety of all new directions, others' and my own.*

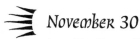 *November 30*

*I would rather walk with God in the dark
than go alone in the light.*

MARY GARDINER BRAINARD

At times, we feel as if we're living through a season
of darkness. During the season of the year when
days are short and there is literally less light, our
feelings may seem to correspond with the darkness
outside of us. We may be grieving what's past or
fearing what lies ahead. We may yearn for deliver-
ance from our particular burdens.

This season of darkness isn't hopeless, but it is
real. We don't have to deny it. Whether darkness
lies outside us or within us, we need to feel it fully—
to feel our losses and griefs, the hurts we and others
suffer, the weight of burdens we are still carrying.
We need to face the truth that there are some aspects of our lives over which we are powerless.

We can acknowledge darkness without letting
it be all there is. Now is the time to remember that
life is precious, friends and loved ones are para-
mount, and a Higher Power is near and ever present. Now is the time to light a candle, to remind
ourselves that there is light as well as darkness.

*Today, I can face darkness,
knowing that it is not all there is.*

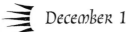 DeceмbeR 1

Having had a spiritual awakening as the result of these steps, . . .

Step Twelve of the
Twelve Steps of Alcoholics Anonymous

Not many of us have had "white light" experiences, in which the purpose of our lives has been revealed to us in a single dramatic instant. For most, awakenings occur as a process over time, as we follow a path of paying attention to our behavior and feelings. When we acknowledge the effects of our actions and understand that we are not alone, we begin to live with greater awareness of reality.

Coming to terms with what we can and can't control, many of us must face the role of addictions in our lives. Whatever our problems, we can become willing to ask other people and a Higher Power for help with what we could not accomplish entirely on our own. Instead of berating ourselves for lack of willpower, equating strength with severity and deprivation, we can seek the support and fellowship of others who share our values and journey. When we are aware that we're part of something larger than our separate, individual egos, our spirits have indeed begun to wake up.

Today, I am willing to be one among many.
I can ask for and offer help.

December 2

*... we tried to carry this message ... and to
practice these principles in all our affairs.*

Step Twelve of the
Twelve Steps of Alcoholics Anonymous

Perhaps our lives have been transformed by coming
out, getting sober, or other life-changing decisions.
We've committed ourselves to the truth of our gay,
lesbian, bisexual, or transgender identities, to principles that illuminate our lives, to actions that work
for us. We've experienced healing and growth, and
we want to spread the word. How do we "carry the
message" so that others can hear it?

People grow and change at their own pace, committing themselves to change when they're ready,
not before. We can't force others to accept our truths
or to change their lives on our timetable. We can
share our experience, strength, and hope, bearing
witness to our own transformation. We can let our
own happiness and clarity serve as an example to
others. We can strengthen our principles through
consistent practice and celebrate our transformation with joy.

*Today, I trust that others have their own timetables
for change and healing. I'm willing to be here for those
who are ready to make use of my experience, strength,
and hope.*

 December 3

One of my worst weaknesses is my pride,
which is just shame in fancy dress.

KAREN DURBIN

What we feel is not always what we show on the
surface. We may have noticed that when others
are self-important, stubborn, or aggressive, they,
too, may be covering feelings of fear, uncertainty,
or low self-esteem. Shame may appear in other
forms—pride, anger, or arrogance—that serve to
disguise true feelings.

We may have been taught to feel shame about
a past occurrence, trait, or feeling. We may feel
shame about an addiction despite living in recovery.
If we have been judged for expressions of a gay, lesbian, bisexual, or transgender identity, early shame
and denial may still remain with us. Whatever our
accomplishments, we may feel, deep down, that
our real selves are not acceptable.

Of what are we still ashamed? Facing our
shame is the beginning of healing. We can bring
into the light any part of ourselves that we may
have disowned or buried. We are worthy of love
and appreciation exactly as we are.

Today, I love and appreciate myself as I am.

December 4

Blessed are the man and the woman
who have grown beyond their greed
and have put an end to their hatred.

PSALM 1:1
translated by Stephen Mitchell

If we believe that someone is our enemy, we ought
to pray with all our hearts for his or her health,
well-being, and happiness; to do this is an act of
healing. Viewing others as our enemies interferes
with our ability to love ourselves. Self-love is not
self-indulgence; it is a gift, one that is necessary for
peace and harmony both within ourselves and
among members of the human family.

In the eyes of a loving Higher Power, we are all
equally lovable. When we accept ourselves exactly
as we are, we can also accept others with their
foibles and differences. Our need to believe that we
are better or worse than someone else evaporates.

When we stop thinking of our lives as some
kind of race, our envy of others' possessions or
success is replaced by generosity. We genuinely
wish others well. We trust that this abundant universe can meet all of our needs for nourishment
and love. Our caring for others opens and frees
our hearts.

Today, I love my life and have no room
in my heart for envy or enmity.

December 5

*Love is not changed by Death, and nothing is lost
and all in the end is harvest.*

EDITH SITWELL

This life we've been given is an opportunity to give
and receive love. There is far more to us and to those
who touch our lives deeply, than our physical bodies. Our energy moves and changes— from spirit to
matter, from matter to spirit. We are all transformed
by love; death does not change that. Instead of clinging to any sense of limitation and loss, we can focus
on the love that continues within us and around us.

Our loving relationships bring us closer to our
own essence and to the essence of Spirit. Love is
not limited by space or time. When our lives have
been touched by love for others, our capacity for
love is enhanced. We can express love in our relationships with the living and with our Higher
Power. We affirm the continuation of love and
let our hearts unfold and blossom in its light.

Today, the light of love lives in me.

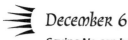 *December 6*

Saying No can be the ultimate self-care.

CLAUDIA BLACK

Learning what our individual preferences and limitations are is an ongoing process of intuition and experience. What is comfortable and desirable for others may be something we ourselves can't safely handle—and may not even want. When we're feeling conflicted about whether or not to follow a friend's lead or to go along with the crowd, we reflect on what we believe. We can ask ourselves if a proposed action is more likely to bring us into closer communication with the spirit within us or to create obstacles to our deep connection with that spirit. We don't have to let fear of the unknown stop us from testing new waters, as long as we're not violating our principles and commitments.

Twelve Step meetings, writing, and conversations with a sponsor, therapist, or trusted friend are some of the many ways we gain access to our intuition, as is going deep within ourselves in prayer and meditation. We can trust our intuition to tell us where we ought to be.

Today, I respect my intuition.

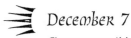

December 7

Change everything except your loves.

VOLTAIRE

Loyalty to the people and principles we care about sustains our spirits and brings us the joy of knowing who we are and why we are here. Our friends and chosen families are precious; with them we can be entirely ourselves. We may change our relationship to gender or sexuality, we may embrace recovery from addictive substances or behavior, we may transform our lives in ways we could not have foreseen—those who care about us delight in these changes that heal and free us.

We, too, delight in our loved ones' transformations. We don't want to limit the growth of those we love. We want fulfillment for others as well as for ourselves. The support we give to and receive from the continuity of loving relationships in our lives helps us to move forward in our process of healing and growth. In the same way, our consistent embrace of principles that have sustained us—the Twelve Steps, for example—empowers us through whatever challenges we face.

Today, I am loyal to my loves,
whether they are people or principles.

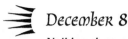

December 8

Nothing gives me the jitters like a bar room full of queers.

WILLIAM BURROUGHS

Whether we experience shyness, self-doubt, or internalized homophobia, many of us fear the very situations that might give us opportunities to find companionship and community. Chances are we're allowing prejudices against others or our own harsh judgment of ourselves to keep us at a safe distance from people who are fundamentally much like ourselves.

We can more easily open our hearts and minds to others when we lower the stakes. Instead of sizing up everyone we meet as a potential lover or life partner, we can begin by considering the possibility of friendship. We can offer warmth and friendliness without having to commit ourselves for a lifetime. We can share information about ourselves and invite others to do the same, respecting our own and others' boundaries, getting to know others through a reassuringly gradual process. We can have fun connecting with others in social situations, instead of fantasizing about perfect relationships as we cling to the supposed safety of isolation.

Today, I step outside myself
and greet another human being.

December 9

*And Ruth said: "Entreat me not to leave thee, or to
return from following after thee; for whither thou
goest I will go; and where thou lodgest, I will lodge:
thy people shall be my people, and thy God my
God; where thou diest, will I die, and there will I
be buried; the Lord do so to me, and more also,
if aught but death part thee and me."*

RUTH 1:16–17

Whether with lovers, friends, or chosen families,
we hope for enduring love that nurtures and supports us. This has been especially challenging for
gay, lesbian, bisexual, and transgender people,
partly because of the stress of living in a homophobic society and partly because of the impact
on our communities of addictions that slow emotional and spiritual growth.

We can develop an understanding of the importance of how we interact with each other, beginning
with clarity about our passions and principles and
affirming those who share them. We can expand
our definition of love, cultivating a larger spirit of
love that supports our common good. We can delight in the love that unites us with those who share
our vision.

*Today, I recognize and further the love
that is all around me.*

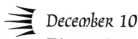 *December 10*

Things are clear only when looked at from a distance.

A. K. RAMANUJAN

At times we feel as if we must make a decision about something in our lives—right now, today. A problem or uncertainty concerning career, home, relationship, or another major area of life confronts us. Our sense of urgency may even spiral into panic as we see first one side of the issue, then the other. How are we to resolve our dilemmas?

When we feel pressured in this way, the best decision we can make is *not* to make any decision. We can wait until we've calmed down emotionally and then let go of the need to decide. When our feelings of urgency and panic quiet down, we will make a decision that's reasonable and right for us.

*Today, I don't have to make decisions under pressure.
I stay in the present and trust that the right choice
will evolve in time, as I am evolving.*

 ## December 11

Connections are made slowly, sometimes they grow underground. You cannot tell always by looking what is happening. More than half a tree is spread out in the soil under your feet.

MARGE PIERCY

"No waiting" is a promise frequently made to us as consumers. We've grown accustomed to fast food and instant communication. Those of us who have struggled with addictive substances and behaviors have been conditioned to expect immediate relief from difficulties.

All of us may need reminding that a solid relationship, effective creative work, integration into a community, and the flowering of our own spirit— whatever truly is worthwhile—take patience as they evolve over time. There are no shortcuts. When we expect instant results in all things, we are bound to be disappointed. The good news is that we can embrace and enjoy every step of a process. If we do our seeding and watering and weeding, the harvest will come in good time. Meanwhile, we can savor the season we are in, cultivating an appreciation of its own particular beauty.

Today, I am patient with myself and my gradual unfolding. I give myself time. I enjoy each step of whatever process I'm engaged in.

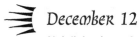 *December 12*

He's living in my head—and he's not even paying rent!

Saying heard in Al-Anon meetings

Each day, each of us has a choice about what we do with the energy of our mind and spirit. We are not required to let an obsession take control of our thoughts.

We can obsess about our desire to have others conform to our ideas and wishes, or we can accept the fact that we cannot control what others think or do. We can cultivate loving detachment in situations involving people with whom we're in conflict, rather than allow disagreement to take over our mental energy. When we're caught up in an obsession, we are no longer living in present reality. Our minds are filled with the numbing repetition of our concern over someone or something beyond our control. We have the choice to come back to the here and now. We don't have to prove others wrong or make certain everyone understands that we're right. We can live and let live—it's freedom.

Today, I don't have room for obsession.
My mind belongs to me.

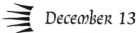

December 13

There are many paths to wisdom, but each begins with a broken heart.

LEONARD COHEN

Our recovery from heartbreak can give us freedom. What we once imagined would be the end of good in our lives can turn out to be the beginning of our maturity and serenity.

Our darkest moments have not destroyed us; they may even have opened doors to greater understanding and aliveness than we could have envisioned. We can look back with tenderness and compassion at the people we once were. We can feel the inner strength and the caring for others that have come from sorrow. We can bear witness to the possibility of survival, healing, and growth. We have the courage to continue on our personal journeys.

Everything I experience serves a purpose. Today, my past is healed; I am alive, awake, and free. I have the courage to change.

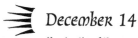 *December 14*

the truth of the new is never on the news

ADRIENNE RICH

Our lives are anything but humdrum. Lesbian, gay, bisexual, and transgender people who are living "out" and people who have embraced Twelve Step recovery from addictions are part of a new consciousness and a new expression of freedom and self-esteem. While not all the old battles are won yet, this time in which we are fortunate to live is allowing us to discover and share what is deep within us. This is a time of healing and creativity.

As individuals, each of us is a unique expression of Spirit; there has never been anyone exactly like us until now. Though we may not often find ourselves represented accurately in the news media, we know that the new reality we are experiencing is shared by members of our communities. We needn't look to outside authorities or old traditions for definitions or explanations of who we are. We can trust our perceptions of our experience.

Today, I am an authority on my own experience.
My life embodies the truth of the new.

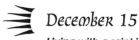

December 15

Living with a saint is more grueling than being one.

ROBERT NEVILLE

Those of us who have come out as gay, lesbian, transgender, or bisexual; who have entered recovery; or who have found a spiritual path that gives meaning and purpose to our lives are deeply fortunate. Let's not make the mistake of alienating our fellow humans by insisting that they follow our example—or worse, by assuming that ours is the only choice that will allow others to flourish.

Respect for difference is something we must accord others as well as ourselves. The decisions that are transforming our lives were not made in an instant; they are the result of many experiences, perhaps of trial and error, perhaps of "hitting bottom" physically or spiritually and having to turn our lives around for our very survival.

We continue to learn and to teach through our mistakes if we're honest about them. Our vulnerabilities and imperfections, far more than preaching or smug self-satisfaction, have the power to touch others. Each of us has our own healing path.

Today, I pray to be useful, as I follow my inner guidance.

December 16

Mending these pale roots of shame,
I find others and break
the chain.

BEATRIX GATES

Participants in Twelve Step programs and in gay, lesbian, bisexual, and transgender communities know that both getting sober and coming out can open doorways to new family. Our families of choice know and care about us, laugh, celebrate, and grieve with us. With them, we need not perpetuate traditions of secrets and shame in fear of forfeiting approval. The opposite is true. The more openly we declare and share who we are, the more surely we are embraced. Our new families appreciate difference—our own and theirs. Together, we acknowledge important moments, creating new traditions and rituals that validate our identities and choices. Together, we break the chains of internalized homophobia, self-rejection, and self-abuse. We no longer feel lonely in the company of others.

Today, I'm healed of shame and secrecy. I am not alone.

December 17

*We moan about not working; and if we get a job
we moan about the director, the script, and the
reviews. If the play's a hit, we moan about the
long run ahead of us. Then we moan because
the play closes and we're out of work.*

DEREK JACOBI

Some of us make almost an art of complaining, finding fault with every change in our circumstances,
whether for good or ill. Nothing ever seems to go the
way we think it should. Even when we get what we
pray for, we immediately begin worrying about tomorrow: what if we can't keep what we have today!

Satisfaction is an active process that requires our
participation; it isn't simply a matter of being given
particular gifts. Some of us are full of gratitude for
a simple meal, others find fault with a banquet. The
difference is less a matter of the menu than of our
attitudes. Satisfaction requires a shift of focus.
When we decide to meet each experience with a
sense of awe and gratitude, we suddenly find ourselves in a generous universe. We are at ease and
content.

*Today, I turn my fears and complaints into gratitude
and awe. I trust the continuing abundance of my life.*

December 18

I do not want to consider my existence merely as one that rises and perishes among the multitude of beings that constitute the universe, but as a life that has value.

ALBERT SCHWEITZER

Fame, material success, high deeds—these are not required for our lives to have value. When we recognize the impact on ourselves and one another of what we choose to say and do, we can live each day with faith that our decisions and actions matter. We and our Higher Power are cocreators of the world.

When we cultivate fear and resentment, we perpetuate states of mind that are limiting to others as well as to ourselves. When we are generous, kind, and happy, we create generosity, kindness, and happiness in those whose lives we touch. What we believe and express as we go through this day has an effect. Our decision to honor the truth of the spirit that moves within us brings the presence of that spirit, and of our Higher Power, into everything we experience.

Today, I listen to the voice of my soul. My life touches other lives as I honor what I know to be true.

Decembeʀ 19

I just had had it with feeling rotten about myself. . . .
It was either change or die, so I died and changed.
SONNY WAINWRIGHT

A fundamental change, no matter how much good
it promises, can frighten us by requiring that we let
go of something that has played a major role in our
past: a habit, a relationship, even a way of thinking
about who we are. We feel the way we imagine a
trapeze artist must feel sailing through space in the
moment between releasing one trapeze and grasp-
ing another.

What awareness, decision, or action have we
feared and avoided? A saying heard in Twelve Step
meetings is "Let go and let God." Some mistakenly
think that this slogan urges a passive approach to
life. Far from it. It recognizes that our work is to
take appropriate actions, not to agonize about outcomes beyond our control. It affirms the participation of a loving Higher Power in our lives as we
address problems, acknowledge our feelings and
deep desires, and remain true to ourselves.

Today, I embrace new life, replacing fear with faith
in the presence of Spirit.

December 20

God made homosexuals, so he must love them.
I love them, too.

SOPHIA LOREN

We are blessed. Our sexual orientation and gender
identity are not willful or rebellious choices, but
embodiments of Spirit. We are who we are by the
grace of a Higher Power.

Our nature as lesbian, gay, bisexual, or transgender people is a gift that we can choose to acknowledge, embrace, and use to increase good in the
world. For many, it functions as an empathetic lens
through which we see and understand others, increasing our compassion for those who experience
oppression. Often, it has been a source of resistance
to that oppression. It has served, too, as an inspiration to originality, as we've reinvented family and
community and created new ways to express our
love for others, ourselves, and our Higher Power. It
has ignited our creative gifts in many areas of expression, quickened our sense of beauty, and made
us healers and bringers of laughter.

Let's see ourselves as worthy of love and praise
the larger love that brought us into existence.

Today, I see myself as the expression of soul.
I appreciate and welcome my unique and loving self.

December 21

What is the greatest hindrance to my achieving serenity? Determination—*the grim resolve that I can* do something *about everything.*

One Day at a Time in Al-Anon

Those of us who have lived with addiction, our own or that of others, may have wished we could control substances or behaviors that deprived us of freedom and serenity. Even those of us who choose to enter recovery may bring with us the desire to maintain a sense of control. The need to fix people, places, and things may be so overwhelming that we lose sight of what is possible for us to accomplish. We may be inappropriately bossy in an effort to take care of other people and problems. We may come to others' rescue whether or not they are ready for our help or want it.

We can learn to respect others' boundaries. We are less likely to attempt to force solutions when we focus on taking appropriate care of ourselves. As we acknowledge the feelings that other people's pain awakens in us, we begin to know more about who we are. We become more available for intimacy and compassion, and thereby help the process of healing.

Today, I don't need to have the answers as I listen to other people's feelings and to my own.

 ## December 22

Even today
my passionate sobriety
is fueled by my
freedom to drink.
I choose not
to.

EILEEN MYLES

Some of us view sobriety as a kind of self-deprivation, one that requires stern resolve and discipline—something that health or morality forces on those who choose it. Instead, we can view it as a person's choice to embrace the life he or she has always wanted, one that embodies freedom and a sense of deep connection to an inner self.

The choice to let go of an addictive substance or behavior is just that—a choice. No one can force it on anyone. If someone is struggling with the appropriateness of choosing recovery, chances are that his or her relationship to addiction needs to be addressed. People rarely raise such questions by accident!

We don't have to struggle. There is no enemy. We can willingly choose, for this day, our desire to live.

Today, I make a free choice to say yes to life.

December 23

*All wars humankind have known have had a
moment which was the beginning of the end.*

NUALA O'FAOLAIN

We may have struggled alone with a personal problem. We look at ourselves as enemies that need to be
conquered. Sometimes we think we've succeeded,
then after a while the problem returns; it seems that
our will cannot conquer it, after all. "The war is
over" is a saying sometimes heard in Twelve Step
recovery meetings. It expresses the relief we feel
when we finally accept the need for help and become ready to give up our embattled resistance.

How are we ever going to reach that readiness
to surrender control and seek help? What others
tell us we ought to do, whether they're close
friends, mentors, or professional experts, is not
enough. It is ultimately our own experience of
"battle fatigue" that tells us we're ready to let go
of a way of life that keeps us always at war with
ourselves. As some put it, "We were sick and tired
of being sick and tired." Asking for help does not
come from a position of weakness, but from the
willingness to listen actively to an inner wisdom
that connects us with our Higher Power.

Today, I am willing to ask for help. I stop battling.

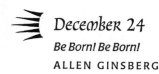

December 24

Be Born! Be Born!

ALLEN GINSBERG

Some new part of us is almost ready to emerge from the chrysalis of this moment. It has been creating itself within our deepest selves. Its womb is woven out of our past days, out of all our experiences—those we've called good and those we've called bad—and out of eternity itself.

This new part of ourselves is full of light that will illuminate whatever we've suffered, whatever we haven't seen or allowed up to now. It may come with weeping; if so, laughter will follow.

We don't have to force it to be born. It will emerge the moment it is ready. Our job is to recognize it, greet it, name it, and celebrate it with joy.

Today, I let the new be born in me.

December 25

Each of us holds the key to the freedom of all of us.
Unlock the truth. Come out.

DEB PRICE

The process of coming out is never entirely finished.
There are always new contexts for reaffirming the
truth of our gay, lesbian, bisexual, and transgender
identities. There are always new elements of those
identities to bring into the light. We discover ever
deeper layers of the truth of who we are, of what we
love and desire, as we continue healing and growing.

The phrase "coming out" suggests going beyond
our private inner conversation and letting our true
selves be seen and heard by others. It evokes courage
as we speak up and live our example despite an environment that may not always seem welcoming. Its
essence is freedom: freedom from secrecy born of
fear, freedom from isolation and a sense of futility.
Its essence is generosity. Our journey of healing and
liberation heals and liberates others.

Today, the truth sets me and others free.

December 26

The true discovery of the intimacy of our ongoing relationship with the Divine can dramatically change our lives.

DAVID A. COOPER

Whether or not we belong to a religious group, whatever our personal beliefs, we can have a daily conversation with Spirit through prayer. We can speak from our hearts in acknowledgment that our lives are a part of something greater than ourselves. We can pray, whether in silence or out loud, in chant or song, alone or in the company of others. We can rest in the moments that sometimes precede prayer: moments of silent awe in the face of nature's power or life's mysterious passages.

Reaching out in prayer begins the process of a relationship. The scope of this relationship extends from our own hidden depths to those of all beings, everywhere. It opens our hearts to the world's love, suffering, and joy. Like all relationships we enter with an open heart, it can create profound changes in our perceptions and in the shape of our lives over time.

Today, I am open to the intimacy of relationship with Spirit through prayer.

December 27

Consider the statements "I am happy" or "I am sad...." They are ... statements of temporary validity. No one is ever permanently happy or sad.... Yet one part of each statement is permanently true: the "I am."

DAVID HARP

Our sense that we exist, apart from other feelings or experiences, has remained with us relatively unchanged since childhood. Whatever we name ourselves, we know that we're alive. Yet, preoccupied as we are with thoughts and sensations, we rarely pay attention to the basic truth of "I am." We can take time to meditate on this simple truth. *We are.*

We ordinarily experience our minds as separate from all others. But we can visualize each individual consciousness as a single drop of water, then imagine it as part of a larger body of water such as a river. In a river, all the drops are connected, part of the same flow.

Through meditation, we can begin to sense our minds' deep connection to the minds of all other living things—one unified body of consciousness. We begin to perceive our own life and mind, our *I am,* as less separate and alone than we previously thought.

Today, I sense my connection to all other beings.

December 28

*Why should it happen that among the great
many women whom I see and am fond of,
suddenly somebody I meet for half an hour
opens the door into poetry?*

MAY SARTON

The world is full of delightful, unpredictable possibilities. We needn't always let habit choose our
path. We can open our eyes to the countless chance
meetings with the unexpected that each day offers.
When we're not preoccupied with our mental routines and obsessions, our minds are alive and awake.
Friends and strangers, familiar and unfamiliar places
can surprise us with sudden flashes of beauty, poetry,
and laughter.

The suggestion is sometimes made in Twelve
Step meetings to "wear the world like a loose gar-
ment." Instead of carrying the weight of the world
on our shoulders, we can let go. We are not responsible for the outcome of every event. We don't have
to fix anyone today, not even ourselves. We can
walk with a lighter step and let ourselves flow into
each moment with ease and pleasure.

Today, I watch for the poetry of the unexpected.

December 29

*I share what and who I am, for I know we
are all one in Spirit.*

LOUISE HAY

With so much attention being paid these days to
the subject of recovery, some of us may wonder
whether or not we qualify to participate in Twelve
Step fellowships. We may think that we—or those
close to us—have a minor problem; we wonder how
it compares with the problems of people in recovery. If the question of addiction has come up for us
or for those whose lives touch ours, it is most likely
something we ought to take a closer look at.

One of the best ways to get at the truth of our
own relationship to addiction is to see whether or
not we identify with the feelings we hear expressed
by people in recovery. We can attend several open
Twelve Step meetings and listen to others share
their experience, strength, and hope. We, too, can
talk honestly with a trusted friend or counselor
about the extent of our concerns. If we listen and
share with an open mind, the answers will come.

*Today, I explore my relationship to addiction by
sharing honestly and listening with an open mind.*

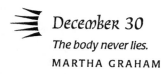

December 30

The body never lies.

MARTHA GRAHAM

Are we hungry for rest, movement, or nourishing food? Are we experiencing pain? Are we attracted to someone? Our bodies are truthful, efficient communicators of both physical and psychological needs and responses. They signal us when we are overtired, angry, and stressed. They tell us, through feelings of tension and relaxation, how we feel about circumstances we're in. They announce our responses to other people. When we say that something is "a pain in the neck," that we're "hot under the collar," or that we have "a gut feeling," we are often telling the literal truth.

As owners of such sophisticated diagnostic equipment, we have the responsibility to care for it lovingly and pay attention to what it tells us. If we get too hungry or tired or if we abuse addictive substances, our bodies send us confused signals. If we find ourselves getting sick, our bodies are letting us know that something is out of balance.

Our bodies are home to our souls in this lifetime. Let's nourish and refresh them appropriately. Let's appreciate their unique beauty and intelligence. Let's listen carefully to what our bodies are telling us.

Today, my body speaks to me and I listen.

December 31

Whenever we get up in the small hours of morning we participate in the monk's praise and enjoyment of dawn. In this liminal place, on the threshold between dream and life, sleep and waking, and darkness and sunshine, we find a special doorway to the spiritual and the eternal.

THOMAS MOORE

It's a new day. I'm awake and breathing. I'm still here with my appetite for life, my gift for seeing and feeling, my visions of love and fulfillment, and my capacity to create myself anew. A day that I once might have given to confusion can instead be a day dedicated to clarity. I'm grateful for the opportunity to greet this glad day, grateful for every day that led me to it. I'm willing to take time to experience its beauty and to appreciate the freedom it offers me to make choices.

I'm in touch with inner selves that I've forgotten or neglected. I trust my ability to nourish myself, body and soul. I know where to seek support and understanding. I pray to serve the Spirit that sustains me and to let my light shine in the world.

Today, I give thanks. I stay alert to opportunities to offer praise and service.

Appendixes

Appendix 1

The Twelve Steps of Alcoholics Anonymous

1. We admitted we were powerless over alcohol—that our lives had become unmanageable.
2. Came to believe that a Power greater than ourselves could restore us to sanity.
3. Made a decision to turn our will and our lives over to the care of God *as we understood Him.*
4. Made a searching and fearless moral inventory of ourselves.
5. Admitted to God, to ourselves, and to another human being the exact nature of our wrongs.
6. Were entirely ready to have God remove all these defects of character.
7. Humbly asked Him to remove our shortcomings.
8. Made a list of all persons we had harmed, and became willing to make amends to them all.
9. Made direct amends to such people wherever possible, except when to do so would injure them or others.
10. Continued to take personal inventory and when we were wrong promptly admitted it.
11. Sought through prayer and meditation to improve our conscious contact with God *as we understood Him,* praying only for knowledge of His will for us and the power to carry that out.
12. Having had a spiritual awakening as the result of these steps, we tried to carry this message to alcoholics, and to practice these principles in all our affairs.

The Twelve Steps of AA are taken from *Alcoholics Anonymous,* 3d ed., published by AA World Services, Inc., New York, N.Y., 59–60. Reprinted with permission of AA World Services, Inc. (See editor's note on copyright page.)

The Twelve Steps of Al-Anon

1. We admitted we were powerless over alcohol—that our lives had become unmanageable.
2. Came to believe that a Power greater than ourselves could restore us to sanity.
3. Made a decision to turn our will and our lives over to the care of God *as we understood Him.*
4. Made a searching and fearless moral inventory of ourselves.
5. Admitted to God, to ourselves, and to another human being the exact nature of our wrongs.
6. Were entirely ready to have God remove all these defects of character.
7. Humbly asked Him to remove our shortcomings.
8. Made a list of all persons we had harmed, and became willing to make amends to them all.
9. Made direct amends to such people wherever possible, except when to do so would injure them or others.
10. Continued to take personal inventory and when we were wrong promptly admitted it.
11. Sought through prayer and meditation to improve our conscious contact with God *as we understood Him,* praying only for knowledge of His will for us and the power to carry that out.
12. Having had a spiritual awakening as the result of these steps, we tried to carry this message to others, and to practice these principles in all our affairs.

Adapted from the Twelve Steps of Alcoholics Anonymous and reprinted with permission of AA World Services, Inc., New York, N.Y., and permission of Al-Anon Family Group Headquarters, Inc., Virginia Beach, Va.

The Twelve Steps of Narcotics Anonymous

1. We admitted that we were powerless over our addiction, that our lives had become unmanageable.
2. We came to believe that a Power greater than ourselves could restore us to sanity.
3. We made a decision to turn our will and our lives over to the care of God *as we understood Him.*
4. We made a searching and fearless moral inventory of ourselves.
5. We admitted to God, to ourselves, and to another human being the exact nature of our wrongs.
6. We were entirely ready to have God remove all these defects of character.
7. We humbly asked Him to remove our shortcomings.
8. We made a list of all persons we had harmed, and became willing to make amends to them all.
9. We made direct amends to such people wherever possible, except when to do so would injure them or others.
10. We continued to take personal inventory and when we were wrong promptly admitted it.
11. We sought through prayer and meditation to improve our conscious contact with God *as we understood Him,* praying only for knowledge of His will for us and the power to carry that out.
12. Having had a spiritual awakening as a result of these steps, we tried to carry this message to addicts, and to practice these principles in all our affairs.

Adapted from the Twelve Steps of Alcoholics Anonymous. Reprinted with permission of AA World Services, Inc., New York, N.Y.

The Twelve Steps of Overeaters Anonymous

1. We admitted we were powerless over food—that our lives had become unmanageable.
2. Came to believe that a Power greater than ourselves could restore us to sanity.
3. Made a decision to turn our will and our lives over to the care of God *as we understood Him.*
4. Made a searching and fearless moral inventory of ourselves.
5. Admitted to God, to ourselves, and to another human being the exact nature of our wrongs.
6. Were entirely ready to have God remove all these defects of character.
7. Humbly asked Him to remove our shortcomings.
8. Made a list of all persons we had harmed, and became willing to make amends to them all.
9. Made direct amends to such people wherever possible, except when to do so would injure them or others.
10. Continued to take personal inventory and when we were wrong, promptly admitted it.
11. Sought through prayer and meditation to improve our conscious contact with God *as we understood Him,* praying only for knowledge of His will for us and the power to carry that out.
12. Having had a spiritual awakening as the result of these steps, we tried to carry this message to compulsive overeaters and to practice these principles in all our affairs.

From *Overeaters Anonymous* ©1980 by Overeaters Anonymous, Inc., Rio Rancho, N. Mex., p. 4. Permission to use the Twelve Steps of Alcoholics Anonymous for adaptation granted by AA World Services, Inc. Reprinted by permission of Overeaters Anonymous, Inc.

The Twelve Suggested Steps
of Sexual Compulsives Anonymous

1. We admitted we were powerless over sexual compulsion—that our lives had become unmanageable.
2. Came to believe that a power greater than ourselves could restore us to sanity.
3. Made a decision to turn our will and our lives over to the care of God, *as we understood God.*
4. Made a searching and fearless moral inventory of ourselves.
5. Admitted to God, to ourselves, and to another human being the exact nature of our wrongs.
6. Were entirely ready to have God remove all these defects of character.
7. Humbly asked God to remove our shortcomings.
8. Made a list of all persons we had harmed and became willing to make amends to them all.
9. Made direct amends to such people wherever possible, except when to do so would injure them or others.
10. Continued to take personal inventory and when we were wrong promptly admitted it.
11. Sought through prayer and meditation to improve our conscious contact with God, *as we understood God,* praying only for knowledge of God's will for us and the power to carry that out.
12. Having had a spiritual awakening as the result of these steps, we tried to carry this message to sexually compulsive people, and to practice these principles in all our affairs.

Adapted from the Twelve Steps of Alcoholics Anonymous. Reprinted with permission of AA World Services, Inc., New York, N.Y. The Twelve Suggested Steps of SCA are taken from *Sexual Compulsives Anonymous: A Program of Recovery,* published by International Service Organization of Sexual Compulsives Anonymous, New York, N.Y., p. 2. Reprinted with permission.

The Twelve Steps of Gamblers Anonymous

1. We admitted we were powerless over gambling—that our lives had become unmanageable.
2. Came to believe that a Power greater than ourselves could restore us to a normal way of thinking and living.
3. Made a decision to turn our will and our lives over to the care of this Power of our own understanding.
4. Made a searching and fearless moral and financial inventory of ourselves.
5. Admitted to God, to ourselves, and to another human being the exact nature of our wrongs.
6. Were entirely ready to have these defects of character removed.
7. Humbly asked God (of our understanding) to remove our shortcomings.
8. Made a list of all persons we had harmed, and became willing to make amends to them all.
9. Made direct amends to such people wherever possible, except when to do so would injure them or others.
10. Continued to take personal inventory and when we were wrong, promptly admitted it.
11. Sought through prayer and meditation to improve our conscious contact with God *as we understood Him,* praying only for knowledge of His will for us and the power to carry that out.
12. Having made an effort to practice these principles in all our affairs, we tried to carry this message to other compulsive gamblers.

Adapted from the Twelve Steps of Alcoholics Anonymous. Reprinted with permission of AA World Services, Inc., New York, N.Y.

Appendix 2

Twelve Step Groups

The following is a partial list of Twelve Step groups:

Alcoholics Anonymous World Services, Inc.
P.O. Box 459
New York, NY 10017-9998

Al-Anon Family Group Headquarters, Inc.
1600 Corporate Landing Parkway
Virginia Beach, VA 23454-5617

Debtors Anonymous
General Service Board
P.O. Box 400
Grand Central Station
New York, NY 10163

Gamblers Anonymous
P.O. Box 17173
Los Angeles, CA 90017

Narcotics Anonymous
P.O. Box 9999
Van Nuys, CA 94109

Overeaters Anonymous
6075 Zenith Ct. NE
Rio Rancho, NM 87124

Sexual Compulsives Anonymous
P.O. Box 1585, Old Chelsea Station
New York, NY 10011

A

abundance, June 2, Oct. 11
acceptance, Aug. 20
acting as if, May 23
action, May 5, May 10, Aug. 13
addiction, Apr. 8, Apr. 29, Aug. 23, Oct. 6, Dec. 29
advice, Feb. 15, Mar. 21, Apr. 16, Oct. 22
affirmations, July 9
ageism, Feb. 11
aging, Apr. 18
amends, Aug. 1
anger, Jan. 16, Feb. 4, Mar. 14, Oct. 15
appreciation, Nov. 29
approval, Oct. 31
argument, Feb. 19, Oct. 23
asking for help, May 12
attention, Mar. 19
attitudes, July 9, Sept. 17
avoiding pain, July 6
awe, Nov. 8

B

balance, Mar. 1
beauty, Jan. 20, Mar. 13, July 16, Oct. 14, Oct. 29,
    Nov. 25
beginnings, Jan. 1, June 4, Oct. 4
being ourselves, Mar. 20
beliefs, Sept. 17
birth, Dec. 24
blaming, Aug. 9
body, Mar. 9, Dec. 30
body image, Feb. 5, Mar. 9

boundaries, Jan. 30, Mar. 4
burnout, July 27

C

celebration, Apr. 5, Apr. 12
celibacy, Feb. 7
centering, May 6, June 10, Aug. 26
change, Feb. 6, Mar. 17, Mar. 18, June 1, July 14,
    Sept. 20, Oct. 24, Dec. 19
children, Jan. 17, Feb. 3
choice, Dec. 22
the closet, May 15
codependency, Sept. 22
coming out, Jan. 3, Dec. 25
communication, Sept. 27
community, Mar. 10, Mar. 23, Mar. 26, Mar. 27,
    May 27
comparisons, Oct. 7
competition, Oct. 11
complexity, May 15, Oct. 24
compulsion, Aug. 29
conformity, Jan. 7
connection, Jan. 14, Mar. 23, Mar. 27, Oct. 2,
    Oct. 19
consistency, Dec. 7
control, Dec. 21
controversy, Jan. 29
cooperation, Mar. 27
courage, Aug. 27, Dec. 19
creativity, Mar. 8, May 26
crisis, Nov. 9

D

darkness, Nov. 30
death, Jan. 25, Mar. 20, June 30, Dec. 5
decisions, May 3, July 3, Nov. 6, Dec. 10
denial, Mar. 15, Apr. 7
detachment, Apr. 20
development, Feb. 2
difference, Apr. 15, May 29, July 10, Aug. 3,
    Aug. 27, Nov. 4, Dec. 15
dignity, May 16
disappointment, Mar. 6, Mar. 22
discipline, June 9, July 12
discrimination, Sept. 14
diversity, Jan. 10
doubt, Apr. 6

E

empowerment, Aug. 18
encouragement, Jan. 22
endings, Jan. 26
enemies, Dec. 4
enthusiasm, July 20
envy, Mar. 5, June 2, Dec. 4
equality, Aug. 21
experience, July 10, Aug. 5, Aug. 19, Dec. 13

F

failure, May 19
faith, May 17, May 23, June 11
fame, Oct. 27
family, Jan. 13, Feb. 1, Mar. 7, May 30, Aug. 14,
    Sept. 5, Nov. 5, Dec. 16

fatigue, July 27
fear, Feb. 17, Mar. 30, May 22
feelings, Jan. 6, June 22, Sept. 11
feminism, July 21
flexibility, May 14
focus on self, June 19, Nov. 22
forgiveness, Mar. 7, May 2, Aug. 25, Sept. 16
freedom, July 12
friendship, Aug. 8, Nov. 17, Dec. 8
fulfillment, Feb. 10

G

generosity, May 20, May 31
geographic cure, Apr. 2, Sept. 29
gifts, June 17
goals, May 19
goodness, Sept. 16
good news, Nov. 23
gratitude, May 7, Dec. 17
grief, Jan. 25, Mar. 22, Oct. 18
guilt, Apr. 10

H

happiness, Sept. 12, Nov. 27
healing, May 28, Aug. 7
helping, Dec. 2
hiding, Jan. 4
Higher Power, Mar. 16, Apr. 3, Apr. 6
history, Feb. 18
HIV/AIDS, Jan. 24, Feb. 21
home, July 23
homophobia, Jan. 31

honoring ourselves, Sept. 18
hope, Apr. 23, July 11
"housecleaning," Feb. 23, Aug. 10, Sept. 6
humility, July 1
humor, Feb. 16, Apr. 17, Nov. 19
hurt, Nov. 13

I

identity, Mar. 29, Apr. 15, Aug. 17
imperfection, Aug. 2
independence, June 21, July 4
individuality, Apr. 28, Aug. 17, Sept. 25
influence, May 25, June 13, July 25
inner authority, Dec. 14
integrity, Nov. 15
intimacy, Aug. 6
intuition, Nov. 21, Dec. 6
invisibility, Aug. 31

J

jealousy, Mar. 5, June 2
joy, June 23, Sept. 11, Oct. 25
judgments, July 30

K

kindness, July 22, Nov. 27

L

language, Mar. 25, July 19
laughter, Jan. 5, Apr. 17, July 17
learning, Jan. 18, Aug. 5

legacies, Aug. 16
letting go, Feb. 23
limitation, Sept. 17
listening, Mar. 11
live and let live, Apr. 16, Dec. 12
loneliness, Mar. 23, Oct. 2
longing, Oct. 3
loss, June 12, Aug. 16, Sept. 13
love, Jan. 12, Jan. 15, Feb. 14, Feb. 21, Apr. 19,
    June 5, July 31, Aug. 20, Sept. 10, Sept. 13,
    Oct. 19, Nov. 16, Dec. 5, Dec. 9, Dec. 20
loyalty, Dec. 7

M

meditation, Apr. 3, June 10, July 18, Sept. 3,
    Sept. 23, Nov. 14, Dec. 27
memory, Apr. 1, June 28, July 8
money, July 26
mothering, June 27
mourning, Nov. 18

N

nature, June 5, July 2
negativity, Oct. 17
newness, May 24, Dec. 24
nurturing, June 27, Oct. 3

O

obsession, July 24, Dec. 12
openness, Aug. 6
originality, June 21
outcomes, Oct. 8

overresponsibility, Feb. 15, June 19, Sept. 22,
    Dec. 21

P

pain, July 6
passivity, Aug. 18
the past, Nov. 11
patience, Feb. 13, May 17, Aug. 4, Nov. 24,
    Dec. 11
peace, Apr. 26, Sept. 15
perfectionism, Apr. 22
persistence, June 4, June 24, Aug. 4
perspective, June 6, Aug. 30
poetry, July 16, Dec. 28
politics, Apr. 11
positiveness, May 8
praise, Nov. 20
prayer, May 23, June 10, Dec. 26, Dec. 31
prejudice, Feb. 28
the present, Sept. 3, Sept. 28
priorities, July 29, Sept. 8, Oct. 22
privacy, May 21
problems, Mar. 22
process, May 5, Oct. 8, Oct. 13, Oct. 18, Dec. 11
progress, Feb. 17, Sept. 20, Oct. 13
purpose, Aug. 12, Sept. 8

Q

questions, May 18
quiet, Aug. 11

R

readiness, Nov. 10
reading, Oct. 30
recovery, June 16, Aug. 23
relationships, Jan. 28, Feb. 20, Mar. 24, Apr. 30,
    June 8, June 26, Sept. 4
renewal, Apr. 4
respect, Oct. 26
responsibility, Feb. 22, Mar. 18, Apr. 29, Sept. 12,
    Oct. 28
risk, Mar. 30, June 20
ritual, Apr. 5
role models, June 13, Jan. 19
routines, June 9

S

safety, June 20, Sept. 7
sanity, Feb. 27, Nov. 28
saying no, Dec. 6
secrets, Apr. 27, Sept. 21, Oct. 9, Nov. 5
self-acceptance, Jan. 2, Apr. 19, Aug. 2, Aug. 27,
    Sept. 2, Sept. 5, Sept. 9, Sept. 30, Oct. 23
self-acknowledgment, Jan. 8
self-care, May 4, June 9
self-disclosure, Nov. 26
self-image, June 18, Aug. 22, Oct. 27, Nov. 12
selfishness, Nov. 22
self-knowledge, Feb. 26, Mar. 29, Apr. 9, June 15,
    June 25
self-love, Jan. 12, Apr. 19, June 14, Dec. 20
self-rejection, Sept. 9
self-sabotage, Feb. 12

self-trust, Feb. 24, Nov. 3
self-worth, May 4, Sept. 25
separatism, Mar. 10
Serenity Prayer, Aug. 30
service, Apr. 13, Apr. 21, July 7
sexuality, Jan. 9, Mar. 28, Oct. 12
shame, Jan. 2, Oct. 21, Dec. 3, Dec. 16
sharing, Mar. 12, May 31, Sept. 21, Dec. 29
shyness, Dec. 8
silence, May 13, July 13, Nov. 7
simplicity, July 29
solitude, Feb. 25
soul, Mar. 24
speaking up, Jan. 21, May 1, May 13, June 3,
    July 28, Sept. 27, Nov. 7
Spirit, July 15, Dec. 31
spiritual awakening, Dec. 1
spirituality, Sept. 19, Nov. 14
spiritual quest, Apr. 9
the Steps:
  in general, June 15
  Step Three, Mar. 16
  Step Four, Apr. 1
  Step Five, May 2
  Step Six, June 1
  Step Seven, July 1
  Step Eight, Aug. 1
  Step Nine, Sept. 1
  Step Ten, Oct. 1
  Step Eleven, Nov. 1, Nov. 2
  Step Twelve, Dec. 1, Dec. 2
stillness, Aug. 11, Aug. 26
stress, Apr. 26

suicide, Oct. 20
support, Oct. 10
surrender, Dec. 23
survival, Jan. 11, Jan. 14, Oct. 5, Dec. 13

T

taking time, Jan. 23, Feb. 29
thoughts, Feb. 8, Oct. 17
tolerance, Feb. 3, Apr. 14, May 25
transformation, Feb. 9, Mar. 2, June 29, Aug. 15
trauma, Aug. 7
trust, Feb. 24
truth, Jan. 17, Mar. 26, Apr. 7, May 11, July 5

U

the unexpected, Dec. 28
unity, Sept. 26, Dec. 27
uprooting, Sept. 6

V

validation, Apr. 25
value, Dec. 18
victimization, Aug. 9
violence, Jan. 27
visibility, Aug. 31

W

walking, Oct. 16
wholeness, May 9, Aug. 24
will, Nov. 2
willingness, Feb. 6, July 14, Dec. 22

witness, Mar. 26, May 11
women, July 21
work, Apr. 24, July 26, Sept. 24
worry, May 22
writing, Mar. 3, May 5

About the Author

JOAN LARKIN is the author of three collections of poetry (*Housework, A Long Sound, Cold River*), a play (*The Living*), and a meditation book (*If You Want What We Have*). She has coedited several anthologies, including *Gay and Lesbian Poetry in Our Time*, which received a Lambda Award. She is the cotranslator of *Sor Juana's Love Poems*. A teacher of writing for many years, she has served on the faculties of Goddard, Brooklyn, and Sarah Lawrence colleges.

About Hazelden Publishing

As part of the Hazelden Betty Ford Foundation, Hazelden Publishing offers both cutting-edge educational resources and inspirational books. Our print and digital works help guide individuals in treatment and recovery, and their loved ones. Professionals who work to prevent and treat addiction also turn to Hazelden Publishing for evidence-based curricula, digital content solutions, and videos for use in schools, treatment programs, correctional programs, and electronic health records systems. We also offer training for implementation of our curricula.

Through published and digital works, Hazelden Publishing extends the reach of healing and hope to individuals, families, and communities affected by addiction and related issues.

For more information about
Hazelden publications, please call **800-328-9000**
or visit us online at **hazelden.org/bookstore.**